HOW TO START AN ECOMMERCE BUSINESS FROM HOME AND QUIT YOUR DAY JOB

A Step-by-Step Guide for Building an Online Store Selling Physical Products

JORDAN MOTIVATOR

TABLE OF CONTENT

INTRODUCTION

Imagine waking up each morning with the freedom to be your own boss, setting your own schedule, and watching your bank account grow as you turn your passion into a profitable venture. In the dynamic landscape of the digital age, the dream of starting a successful ecommerce business from the comfort of your home has never been more attainable.

Did you know that ecommerce sales are projected to surpass $6.54 trillion by 2022, accounting for a significant portion of global retail?

This statistic not only reflects the tremendous growth potential within the ecommerce industry but also underscores a transformative shift in the way people shop and do business. If you've ever dreamt of breaking free from the nine-to-five grind, reclaiming control Omover your time, and unlocking financial independence, you're not alone. Many share the same aspirations but often find themselves paralyzed by the complexities and uncertainties that come with launching an ecommerce venture.

The Problem:

You might be grappling with questions like:

How do I find a profitable niche in a crowded market?

What steps do I need to take to set up a reliable and secure online store?

How can I effectively market my products and stand out from the competition?

Is it really possible to turn my passion into a sustainable source of income and eventually quit my day job?

The journey to ecommerce success is riddled with challenges, and it's easy to feel overwhelmed and uncertain about where to begin. However, the good news is that you've taken the first step by picking up this book.

The Solution:

Welcome to "How to Start an Ecommerce Business from Home and Quit Your Day Job." This book is not just a guide; it's a roadmap that will navigate you through the intricacies of starting and growing a thriving online business. Whether you're a budding entrepreneur or someone looking to diversify income streams, this book is crafted to address your pain points, eliminate confusion, and empower you with the knowledge and strategies needed to turn your ecommerce dream into a reality.

Key Topics:

Here is a sneak peek at what to expect:

Discovering your niche and passion

Crafting a solid business plan and setting achievable goals

Building a user-friendly website and selecting the right platform

Effectively marketing your products in the digital landscape

Navigating inventory management and implementing efficient fulfillment strategies

Scaling your business for long-term success

Are you prepared to set out on a path that has the power to change your life? Keep reading, and let's explore the exciting world of ecommerce together. By the end of this book, you'll not only possess the knowledge to start your own online business but also have the confidence to say goodbye to your day job and embrace the freedom of being a successful ecommerce entrepreneur. Your journey begins now.

Welcome to the World of

Ecommerce

In the vast and ever-evolving landscape of business, the digital realm has emerged as a revolutionary force, reshaping the way commerce is conducted. Welcome to the World of Ecommerce, a dynamic space where innovation, technology, and entrepreneurship converge to redefine how products and services reach consumers.

In this exhilarating world, geographical boundaries fade away, and marketplaces span the entire globe. The traditional barriers that once restricted businesses are dismantled, opening doors for anyone with a dream and a digital connection to participate in the global marketplace. Ecommerce transcends the limitations of brick-and-mortar establishments, allowing entrepreneurs to establish and grow businesses from the comfort of their homes.

Breaking Down the Walls:

Gone are the days when starting a business required a physical storefront, significant capital, and a myriad of logistical challenges. Today, the World of Ecommerce beckons, inviting individuals with diverse passions and skills to carve their niche in the digital landscape. Whether you're an artist, a tech enthusiast, or a connoisseur of unique goods, ecommerce provides a platform for your creations to find a home and an audience.

The Power of Connectivity:

Ecommerce isn't just a marketplace; it's a global community where businesses, big and small, connect with consumers seeking unique products and personalized experiences. With a few clicks, customers can explore a universe of offerings, compare prices, read reviews, and make informed decisions. The power lies not only in the variety of products available but also in the ability to connect with brands that resonate with personal values and aspirations.

Embracing Innovation:

Welcome to an ecosystem that thrives on innovation and adapts to technological advancements. From artificial intelligence enhancing customer experiences to blockchain securing transactions, the World of Ecommerce is at the forefront of technological evolution. Entrepreneurs are empowered to leverage these tools, providing seamless, secure, and personalized experiences for their customers.

Your Journey Begins Here:

As you step into the World of Ecommerce, envision the possibilities that lie ahead. This space is not just about transactions; it's about creating, connecting, and transforming. Whether you're an aspiring entrepreneur or a seasoned business owner looking to expand your horizons, the opportunities are boundless.

This book serves as your guide, unveiling the secrets, strategies, and insights needed to navigate and succeed in the World of Ecommerce. Together, let's embark on a journey that transcends geographical constraints, defies traditional business models, and welcomes you into the vibrant and transformative world of digital commerce. Welcome, and let the adventure begin!

The Promise of Financial Freedom

The Promise of Financial Freedom:

In the realm of Ecommerce, the pursuit of financial freedom is not just a lofty aspiration; it's a tangible promise awaiting those willing to embark on the journey. The allure of financial freedom has the power to transform lives, redefine priorities, and open doors to a future where individuals are not bound by the constraints of traditional employment.

Breaking Free from Financial Constraints:

At the heart of the promise lies the liberation from financial constraints that often accompany conventional career paths. The World of Ecommerce introduces a paradigm shift where your income is not tethered to the conventional limitations of a 9-to-5 job. Instead, it invites you to take control of your financial destiny, presenting opportunities to generate income that transcends the boundaries of time and location.

Creating Multiple Streams of Income:

Ecommerce empowers entrepreneurs to diversify their revenue streams, a key principle in achieving financial freedom. By building and scaling an online business, individuals can create multiple avenues for income, reducing dependency on a single source. Whether through product sales, affiliate marketing, or other innovative strategies, the promise of financial freedom lies in the ability to cultivate a resilient and sustainable income portfolio.

Flexibility and Autonomy:

The promise of financial freedom is intricately tied to the flexibility and autonomy that Ecommerce affords. As an ecommerce entrepreneur, you have the power to set your own schedule, decide your work environment, and choose the projects that align with your passions. This autonomy not only enhances work-life balance but also contributes to the overarching goal of achieving financial independence.

Building Long-Term Wealth:

Ecommerce offers a unique avenue for building long-term wealth. The scalable nature of online businesses allows for exponential growth over time, providing a pathway to accumulating assets and securing a financial future. By implementing sound financial management practices and leveraging the potential of a thriving ecommerce venture, individuals can create a legacy of prosperity for themselves and their families.

Embracing the Journey:

The promise of financial freedom is not a guaranteed outcome but a result of dedication, strategic planning, and a willingness to embrace the challenges inherent in entrepreneurship. As you delve into the intricacies of the Ecommerce landscape, remember that each step you take brings you closer to the realization of this promise.

This book is your guide, offering insights, strategies, and practical advice to navigate the complexities of Ecommerce and unlock the promise of financial freedom. Whether you seek to supplement your income, escape the limitations of traditional employment, or build a legacy of wealth, the journey begins with the decision to explore the boundless possibilities within the World of Ecommerce. Embrace the promise, and let the pursuit of financial freedom be the driving force propelling you toward a brighter and more empowered future.

Is Ecommerce Right for You?

Embarking on an ecommerce journey is an exciting prospect, but it's crucial to assess whether this dynamic and ever-evolving field aligns with your aspirations, skills, and lifestyle. Before diving into the intricacies of online business, consider the following questions to determine if ecommerce is the right fit for you.

Passion and Interest:

Question: Are you passionate about a particular product or niche?

Consideration: Ecommerce often thrives when driven by passion. Choosing a niche or product you genuinely care about not only sustains motivation during challenges but also helps you connect with your target audience on a personal level.

Adaptability:

Question: Are you comfortable adapting to technological advancements and market trends?

Consideration: Ecommerce is a fast-paced environment where staying current with technology, consumer behavior, and industry trends is essential. If you enjoy adapting to change and learning new skills, ecommerce might be an ideal fit.

Risk Tolerance:

Question: How comfortable are you with taking calculated risks?

Consideration: Like any entrepreneurial endeavor, ecommerce involves risks. Understanding and managing risks is crucial. If you are open to calculated risks and possess resilience in the face of setbacks, ecommerce may be well-suited for you.

Time Commitment:

Question: Can you commit time to the consistent growth of your ecommerce venture?

Consideration: Successful ecommerce businesses require time and effort. While the flexibility of working from home is a perk, a commitment to consistent effort, especially in the initial stages, is vital for long-term success.

Independence:

Question: Do you enjoy working independently and making decisions autonomously?

Consideration: Ecommerce entrepreneurs often have the autonomy to make critical decisions for their businesses. If you thrive in an independent work environment and enjoy the freedom to shape your own path, ecommerce may be a perfect match.

Customer Focus:

Question: Are you customer-oriented and willing to prioritize their needs?

Consideration: Customer satisfaction is at the core of ecommerce success. If you enjoy creating positive customer experiences and are willing to go the extra mile to meet their needs, you'll likely find fulfillment in the ecommerce space.

Long-Term Vision:

Question: Do you have a long-term vision for your business?

Consideration: Ecommerce is not just about immediate gains; it's about building a sustainable and scalable business. If you have a vision for the long-term growth and development of your venture, ecommerce could be a fitting choice.

Conclusion:

Assessing whether ecommerce is right for you involves a thoughtful examination of your interests, strengths, and aspirations. This book aims to guide you through the process, providing insights, strategies, and practical advice to help you make informed decisions on your journey into the world of ecommerce. If you find resonance with the considerations above, then the exciting and transformative world of ecommerce may very well be the perfect match for your entrepreneurial ambitions.

Chapter 1: Understanding Ecommerce

Defining Ecommerce and Its Types

In a world where digital connectivity shapes the way we live, shop, and do business, Electronic Commerce, commonly known as Ecommerce, stands as a transformative force. At its core, Ecommerce refers to the buying and selling of goods and services over the internet. This revolutionary approach to commerce has not only redefined traditional business models but has also empowered entrepreneurs and consumers alike.

Understanding Ecommerce:

B2C (Business-to-Consumer):

Definition: B2C ecommerce involves transactions between a business and individual consumers.

Example: Online retail platforms, such as Amazon or Etsy, where consumers purchase products directly from businesses.

B2B (Business-to-Business):

Definition: B2B ecommerce focuses on transactions between businesses, where one business sells products or services to another.

Example: Wholesale platforms or marketplaces connecting manufacturers with retailers.

C2C (Consumer-to-Consumer):

Definition: C2C ecommerce involves transactions between individual consumers, often facilitated by an online platform.

Example: Online marketplaces like eBay or Poshmark, where individuals buy and sell secondhand goods.

C2B (Consumer-to-Business):

Definition: C2B ecommerce occurs when individual consumers sell products or services to businesses.

Example: Influencers or freelancers offering their services to businesses through platforms like Upwork or Fiverr.

Types of Ecommerce Models:

Traditional Ecommerce:

Definition: Involves online transactions for physical goods, resembling the traditional retail model.

Example: Online stores selling clothing, electronics, or any tangible product.

Digital Products Ecommerce:

Definition: Focuses on the sale of digital goods or services that can be downloaded or accessed online.

Example: Platforms selling e-books, software, music, or online courses.

Subscription Ecommerce:

Definition: Customers pay a recurring fee to access products or services regularly.

Example: Subscription boxes for beauty products, meal kits, or streaming services like Netflix.

Service-based Ecommerce:

Definition: Involves the online delivery of services rather than physical goods.

Example: Online consultation services, virtual classes, or freelance platforms.

Advantages of Ecommerce:

Global Reach:

Geographical restrictions are irrelevant with e-commerce, giving companies access to a worldwide customer base.

24/7 Accessibility:

Online stores operate round the clock, providing customers with the flexibility to shop at any time.

Cost Efficiency:

Lower overhead costs compared to brick-and-mortar stores, enabling businesses to offer competitive prices.

Data-driven Insights:

Ecommerce platforms generate valuable data that businesses can use to understand consumer behavior and optimize strategies.

Conclusion:

Defining Ecommerce goes beyond mere transactions; it represents a shift in the way businesses connect with consumers and deliver value. This book will delve deeper into the intricacies of each Ecommerce type, providing insights and strategies to help you navigate the diverse landscape of digital commerce successfully. Whether you're a budding entrepreneur or a seasoned business owner, understanding the nuances of Ecommerce is the key to unlocking its vast potential.

Ecommerce Trends and Opportunities

In the ever-evolving landscape of digital commerce, staying abreast of emerging trends is paramount for entrepreneurs seeking to capitalize on opportunities and navigate the competitive terrain. The dynamic nature of Ecommerce ensures that trends are not static; they shift, adapt, and open doors to innovative possibilities. Let's explore some current Ecommerce trends and the exciting opportunities they present.

Mobile Commerce (M-commerce):

Trend: The increasing prevalence of smartphones has propelled the rise of mobile commerce.

Opportunity: Optimize your Ecommerce platform for mobile users, invest in mobile apps, and leverage technologies like mobile wallets for seamless transactions.

Personalization and AI:

Trend: AI-driven algorithms analyze customer data to provide personalized recommendations and experiences.

Opportunity: Implement AI tools to understand customer behavior, personalize product recommendations, and enhance the overall shopping experience.

Sustainable Ecommerce:

Trend: Consumers are increasingly prioritizing sustainable and eco-friendly products.

Opportunity: Embrace sustainability by offering eco-friendly products, transparent supply chains, and environmentally conscious practices.

Voice Commerce:

Trend: The adoption of voice-activated devices is influencing how consumers make online purchases.

Opportunity: Optimize your website for voice search, explore voice-activated shopping features, and stay attuned to developments in voice technology.

Augmented Reality (AR) and Virtual Reality (VR):

Trend: AR and VR technologies enhance the online shopping experience by allowing customers to visualize products.

Opportunity: Integrate AR features for virtual product try-ons, 360-degree views, or interactive experiences to boost customer engagement.

Subscription-based Models:

Trend: The subscription model offers convenience and recurring revenue for both products and services.

Opportunity: Explore subscription-based offerings, such as curated boxes, memberships, or regular product replenishment services.

Social Commerce:

Trend: Social media platforms are increasingly becoming channels for direct Ecommerce transactions.

Opportunity: Leverage social commerce by integrating shoppable posts, utilizing social media ads, and engaging with customers on platforms like Instagram and Facebook.

Blockchain Technology:

Trend: Blockchain enhances transparency and security in transactions and supply chains.

Opportunity: Explore blockchain applications to build trust, secure transactions, and ensure the authenticity of products.

Contactless Payments:

Trend: The preference for contactless payments has accelerated, especially in the wake of global events.

Opportunity: Offer a variety of secure and contactless payment options to cater to changing consumer preferences.

Chatbots and Customer Service Automation:

Trend: AI-driven chatbots provide instant customer support and assistance.

Opportunity: Implement chatbots for real-time customer interactions, order tracking, and addressing frequently asked questions.

Conclusion:

Ecommerce is a dynamic ecosystem where trends not only reflect consumer preferences but also create vast opportunities for innovation and growth. By staying informed about these trends and proactively adapting your Ecommerce strategy, you position yourself to capitalize on emerging opportunities and build a resilient and future-proof online business. This book will delve deeper into these trends, providing insights and strategies to help you harness the full potential of Ecommerce in the current and future digital landscape.

Benefits and Challenges of Ecommerce

commerce, the digital frontier of commerce, has reshaped the way businesses operate and consumers shop. As with any transformative paradigm, there are both considerable benefits and unique challenges associated with embracing the world of online commerce.

Benefits of Ecommerce:

Global Reach:

Benefit: Ecommerce transcends geographical boundaries, providing businesses with access to a global market.

Implication: Reach diverse audiences, expand your customer base, and tap into international markets without the constraints of a physical storefront.

24/7 Accessibility:

Benefit: Online stores operate around the clock, offering customers the flexibility to shop at any time.

Implication: Capture sales from different time zones, cater to varied schedules, and provide a seamless shopping experience irrespective of traditional business hours.

Cost Efficiency:

Benefit: Ecommerce often requires lower overhead costs compared to brick-and-mortar establishments.

Implication: Reduce expenses related to physical space, personnel, and utilities, allowing businesses to offer competitive prices to consumers.

Data-Driven Insights:

Benefit: Ecommerce platforms generate valuable data on customer behavior, preferences, and purchasing patterns.

Implication: Leverage data analytics to make informed decisions, personalize marketing strategies, and continually optimize the customer experience.

Increased Customer Engagement:

Benefit: Ecommerce platforms facilitate direct and instant communication with customers.

Implication: Engage with customers through newsletters, social media, and personalized promotions, fostering brand loyalty and building lasting relationships.

Diverse Revenue Streams:

Benefit: Ecommerce enables the creation of multiple revenue streams through various products, services, or affiliate marketing.

Implication: Diversify income sources to create a more resilient business model and adapt to changing market conditions.

Challenges of Ecommerce:

Security Concerns:

Challenge: Ecommerce transactions involve sensitive customer information, making security a top concern.

Consideration: Implement robust security measures, encryption, and compliance with data protection regulations to ensure customer trust.

Intense Competition:

Challenge: The ease of entry into the ecommerce market contributes to heightened competition.

Consideration: Develop a unique value proposition, focus on brand differentiation, and continually innovate to stay ahead in the competitive landscape.

Logistical Complexities:

Challenge: Managing inventory, order fulfillment, and shipping can be complex, especially for growing businesses.

Consideration: Implement efficient inventory management systems, explore reliable shipping partners, and optimize supply chain processes.

Technical Issues:

Challenge: Ecommerce platforms may face technical glitches, leading to issues with website functionality.

Consideration: Regularly update and maintain the website, conduct thorough testing, and provide responsive customer support to address technical issues promptly.

Customer Trust and Experience:

Challenge: Establishing trust in an online environment and providing a positive customer experience is crucial.

Consideration: Prioritize user-friendly website design, transparent communication, and responsive customer service to build and maintain trust.

Regulatory Compliance:

Challenge: Ecommerce businesses must adhere to various regulations and legal requirements.

Consideration: Stay informed about relevant laws, privacy policies, and industry standards to ensure compliance and mitigate legal risks.

Conclusion:

Ecommerce offers a multitude of benefits, empowering businesses to reach a global audience, operate efficiently, and thrive in the digital age. However, navigating the challenges is essential for sustained success. By understanding and addressing these challenges proactively, businesses can harness the full potential of ecommerce, providing customers with a seamless and secure online shopping experience. This book will delve deeper into strategies to maximize benefits and overcome challenges, ensuring a well-rounded understanding of the dynamic world of ecommerce.

Chapter 2: Finding Your Niche

Identifying Your Passion and Expertise

Embarking on the journey of starting an ecommerce business from home requires more than just a product or a service; it demands a genuine connection with your venture. Before delving into the technicalities of online entrepreneurship, take the time to identify your passion and expertise, as they form the cornerstone of a successful and fulfilling ecommerce venture.

Unveiling Your Passion:

Self-Reflection:

Process: Reflect on your interests, hobbies, and the activities that bring you joy.

Outcome: Identifying a passion aligns your business with something you love, ensuring sustained motivation and enthusiasm.

Solving a Problem:

Process: Consider the challenges you've faced or observed around you.

Outcome: Aligning your business with solving real problems not only fuels passion but also adds inherent value to your offerings.

What Would You Do for Free?

Process: Imagine a scenario where money is not a factor. What activities or work would you willingly engage in?

Outcome: Identifying activities you are willing to do for free often unveils your true passions and interests.

Leveraging Your Expertise:

Professional Background:

Assessment: Evaluate your professional background, education, and work experience.

Outcome: Your expertise in a particular field can provide a solid foundation for an ecommerce business.

Skills Inventory:

Assessment: List down your skills, both hard and soft, that can be applied to a business.

Outcome: Recognizing your skill set helps in aligning your expertise with potential business opportunities.

Market Demand:

Research: Explore market trends and identify areas where there is a demand for specific skills or knowledge.

Outcome: Aligning your expertise with market demand enhances the viability of your ecommerce venture.

The Intersection of Passion and Expertise:

Finding Common Ground:

Alignment: Look for the intersection between your passion and your expertise.

Outcome: A business rooted in both passion and expertise stands a higher chance of long-term success and personal fulfillment.

Addressing a Niche:

Specialization: Identify a niche within your passion and expertise.

Outcome: Specialization allows you to stand out in a crowded market and cater to a specific audience.

Continuous Learning:

Commitment: Stay committed to continuous learning within your chosen niche.

Outcome: Keeping up with industry trends ensures that your expertise remains relevant and valuable.

Conclusion:

Identifying your passion and expertise is not just the first step; it's the foundation upon which your ecommerce venture will flourish. It's the driving force that will propel you through challenges and inspire creativity and innovation. Take the time to explore your passions, leverage your expertise, and find that sweet spot where your personal fulfillment aligns with a market need. This book will guide you in channeling that passion and expertise into a thriving ecommerce business that not only meets your financial goals but also brings you joy and satisfaction.

Researching Profitable Ecommerce Niches

One of the critical steps in launching a successful ecommerce business is identifying a profitable niche. A niche is a specialized segment of the market that caters to a specific audience with distinct needs or interests. Effective niche selection is a cornerstone of a thriving online venture, offering the potential for reduced competition and increased customer loyalty. Here's a guide on how to research and identify lucrative ecommerce niches.

Personal Interests and Hobbies:

Exploration: Start by exploring your own interests, hobbies, and passions.

Consideration: Your personal connection to a niche can fuel enthusiasm and provide valuable insights into market demands.

Market Demand Analysis:

Research: Conduct thorough market research to identify current trends and demands.

Tools: Utilize keyword research tools, Google Trends, and industry reports to understand what products or services are currently in demand.

Competition Analysis:

Evaluation: Analyze the level of competition within potential niches.

Consideration: Lower competition doesn't mean no competition; assess if you can differentiate your offering within the existing market.

Target Audience Identification:

Define: Clearly define your target audience and their demographics.

Insight: Understanding your audience's needs and preferences helps tailor your niche to meet specific requirements.

Solve a Problem:

Identification: Look for problems or challenges within a niche that you can address.

Value Proposition: Offering solutions to problems can create a unique value proposition that attracts customers.

Evaluate Profit Margins:

Analysis: Assess the potential profit margins within different niches.

Consideration: A high demand for a product or service does not guarantee profitability; ensure that the niche offers viable profit margins.

Seasonal Trends and Evergreen Niches:

Understanding: Distinguish between seasonal trends and evergreen niches.

Strategy: Seasonal trends may offer quick bursts of revenue, while evergreen niches provide more stable, long-term opportunities.

Check Social Media Trends:

Observation: Monitor social media platforms for emerging trends and discussions.

Insight: Social media can offer real-time insights into what products or services are gaining popularity.

Evaluate Legal and Regulatory Aspects:

Investigation: Research any legal or regulatory considerations specific to potential niches.

Mitigation: Ensure compliance with industry regulations and legal requirements to avoid future complications.

Passion vs. Profitability:

Balance: Find a balance between personal passion and the potential profitability of a niche.

Objective Assessment: Be objective in assessing whether your passion aligns with a niche that has genuine market demand.

Test and Validate:

Prototyping: Consider testing a small-scale version of your product or service.

Feedback: Gather feedback and validate your niche's potential before committing to a full-scale launch.

Conclusion:

Researching profitable ecommerce niches requires a combination of personal interest, market analysis, and a keen understanding of your target audience. By carefully evaluating market trends, competition, and potential profitability, you can uncover lucrative opportunities within a niche that aligns with your passions and business goals. This book will guide you through the process, providing strategies and insights to help you identify and capitalize on a niche that not only resonates with your interests but also ensures the success of your ecommerce venture.

Analyzing Market Demand and Competition

Before launching an ecommerce venture, a comprehensive analysis of market demand and competition is essential. Understanding the dynamics of the market ensures that your business is well-positioned to meet customer needs and effectively navigate the competitive landscape. Here's a guide on how to analyze market demand and competition for your ecommerce niche.

Conducting Market Research:

Purpose: Gather information about your target market, potential customers, and their preferences.

Methods: Utilize surveys, interviews, and online research tools to collect relevant data.

Identifying Customer Needs:

Focus: Understand the specific needs and pain points of your target audience.

Outcome: Tailor your products or services to address these needs, ensuring a strong market fit.

Utilizing Keyword Research:

Tool Usage: Leverage keyword research tools to identify popular search terms related to your niche.

Insight: Analyze the volume and competitiveness of keywords to gauge market interest.

Competitor Analysis:

Identification: Identify and analyze key competitors in your niche.

Focus Areas: Evaluate their product offerings, pricing strategies, marketing approaches, and customer reviews.

SWOT Analysis:

Assessment: Conduct a SWOT analysis (Strengths, Weaknesses, Opportunities, Threats) for your business and competitors.

Insight: Understand your competitive advantages and potential areas for improvement.

Market Trends and Insights:

Observation: Stay informed about industry trends, emerging technologies, and changing consumer behaviors.

Adaptation: Adapt your business strategies based on evolving market dynamics to stay relevant.

Evaluate Pricing Strategies:

Comparison: Analyze the pricing strategies of competitors offering similar products or services.

Value Proposition: Determine how your pricing aligns with market expectations and the perceived value of your offerings.

Customer Feedback and Reviews:

Collection: Gather customer feedback and reviews on your competitors and similar products in the market.

Learning: Identify areas where competitors excel or fall short, providing insights for your business strategy.

Identify Market Gaps:

Gap Analysis: Determine if there are unmet needs or gaps in the market that your business can address.

Innovation: Explore opportunities to innovate and differentiate your offerings based on these gaps.

Assessing Market Size and Growth:

Research: Determine the overall size of your target market and its growth potential.

Strategic Planning: Use this information to guide your strategic planning and set realistic business goals.

Evaluate Distribution Channels:

Channel Analysis: Analyze the distribution channels your competitors are using.

Optimization: Optimize your distribution strategy based on the most effective channels for reaching your target audience.

Regulatory and Legal Considerations:

Research: Understand any regulatory or legal considerations relevant to your ecommerce niche.

Compliance: Ensure that your business operations comply with all applicable regulations.

Conclusion:

Analyzing market demand and competition provides a solid foundation for your ecommerce business. By gaining insights into customer needs, competitor strategies, and overall market dynamics, you can make informed decisions, refine your offerings, and develop effective marketing strategies. This book will guide you through the process, offering practical tips and strategies to help you analyze and leverage market demand and competition effectively in the dynamic world of ecommerce.

Chapter 3: Creating a Business Plan

The Importance of a Solid Business Plan

In the dynamic and competitive landscape of ecommerce, having a solid business plan is not just a formality; it is a strategic roadmap that can significantly impact the success and sustainability of your venture. A well-crafted business plan serves as a guide, outlining your goals, strategies, and the steps you need to take to achieve them. Here's why having a solid business plan is crucial for your ecommerce journey:

Clear Roadmap for Success:

Direction: A business plan provides a clear roadmap, outlining your business goals and the steps to achieve them.

Guidance: It serves as a guiding document, helping you navigate challenges and make informed decisions throughout your entrepreneurial journey.

Understanding Your Market:

Market Analysis: A business plan includes a thorough analysis of your target market, helping you understand customer needs, preferences, and market trends.

Insight: This insight is crucial for tailoring your products or services to meet market demands effectively.

Setting Realistic Goals:

Goal Definition: Through a business plan, you define realistic and measurable goals for your ecommerce business.

Motivation: Clear goals provide motivation for both you and your team, driving focused efforts toward achieving milestones.

Attracting Investors and Partners:

Professionalism: Investors and potential partners often require a business plan to assess the viability and potential of your business.

Confidence: A well-prepared business plan instills confidence in stakeholders, showcasing your commitment and strategic thinking.

Financial Planning and Management:

Budgeting: A business plan includes financial projections, helping you budget effectively and allocate resources strategically.

Risk Mitigation: It allows you to identify potential financial challenges and plan for risk mitigation.

Operational Efficiency:

Workflow Optimization: Your business plan outlines operational processes, ensuring a smooth workflow and efficient resource utilization.

Adaptability: It allows you to adapt and refine operations based on changing market conditions or internal dynamics.

Brand Positioning and Marketing Strategies:

Brand Definition: A business plan helps define your brand positioning and unique selling propositions.

Marketing Guidelines: It outlines marketing strategies, ensuring a consistent and effective approach to promoting your ecommerce business.

Risk Management:

Identification: A solid business plan identifies potential risks and challenges that your business may face.

Mitigation Strategies: It enables you to develop proactive strategies to mitigate risks, enhancing the resilience of your ecommerce venture.

Resource Allocation:

Efficient Resource Use: Through financial projections and operational plans, a business plan aids in efficient resource allocation.

Prioritization: It helps prioritize tasks, investments, and activities based on their impact on overall business objectives.

Adaptability and Flexibility:

Strategic Adjustments: While providing a structured plan, a business plan allows for adaptability and strategic adjustments.

Response to Changes: It equips you to respond to market changes, technological advancements, and unexpected events with agility.

Conclusion:

A solid business plan is not just a static document; it is a living blueprint that evolves with your business. It guides your decisions, instills confidence in stakeholders, and provides a foundation for success. Whether you're a startup entrepreneur or a seasoned business owner entering the ecommerce space, investing time and effort into crafting a comprehensive business plan is an invaluable step towards building a resilient and successful online business. This book will guide you through the process, offering insights and practical advice to help you develop a business plan that propels your ecommerce venture to new heights.

Defining Your Unique Selling Proposition (USP)

In the competitive landscape of ecommerce, establishing a Unique Selling Proposition (USP) is paramount to differentiate your brand and capture the attention of your target audience. Your USP is the distinctive factor that sets your business apart from competitors and convinces customers to choose your products or services. Here's a guide on how to define your Unique Selling Proposition:

Understand Your Target Audience:

Analysis: Conduct a thorough analysis of your target audience, including their needs, preferences, and pain points.

Insight: Understanding your audience is crucial for tailoring your USP to resonate with their specific desires.

Identify Your Competitors:

Analysis: Identify key competitors in your niche and analyze their offerings and messaging.

Differentiation: Identify gaps or areas where you can differentiate your business from competitors.

Highlight Your Strengths:

Self-Reflection: Reflect on the strengths and unique aspects of your business.

Emphasis: Your USP should emphasize what you do exceptionally well and why customers should choose you.

Address Customer Pain Points:

Feedback: Gather customer feedback and identify common pain points within your niche.

Solution: Position your USP as the solution to these pain points, demonstrating how your offerings address specific customer needs.

Quality and Innovation:

Emphasis on Quality: If your products excel in quality, make it a central part of your USP.

Innovation: If innovation is a strength, showcase how your products or services bring something new and valuable to the market.

Emphasize Benefits, Not Just Features:

Customer-Centric: Focus on how your products or services benefit the customer, rather than just listing features.

Value Proposition: Clearly communicate the value customers will gain by choosing your brand.

Unique Offerings or Exclusivity:

Exclusive Products: If applicable, emphasize exclusive products or services that customers can only get from your brand.

Limited Editions: Create a sense of exclusivity by offering limited editions or unique variants.

Customer Experience:

Service Excellence: If exceptional customer service is a strength, incorporate it into your USP.

Ease of Transactions: Highlight features that enhance the overall customer experience, such as user-friendly interfaces or hassle-free transactions.

Craft a Compelling Slogan or Tagline:

Memorability: Develop a memorable slogan or tagline that encapsulates your USP.

Conciseness: Keep it concise but impactful, conveying the essence of your brand in a few words.

Consistent Branding Across Platforms:

Brand Identity: Ensure that your USP is consistently communicated across all platforms.

Visual Elements: Incorporate your USP into visual elements, such as logos and branding, to reinforce brand identity.

Test and Iterate:

Feedback Loop: Test your USP with a sample audience and gather feedback.

Refinement: Use the feedback to refine and iterate your USP for maximum effectiveness.

Transparency and Authenticity:

Honesty: Be transparent and authentic in your communication.

Trust Building: Build trust by aligning your actions with the promises made in your USP.

Conclusion:

Defining your Unique Selling Proposition is a strategic process that requires a deep understanding of your market, competitors, and, most importantly, your customers. A compelling USP not only differentiates your brand but also forms the foundation for effective marketing and brand loyalty. This book will guide you through the steps of defining and leveraging your USP, providing insights and practical tips to help your ecommerce business stand out in a crowded marketplace.

Setting Realistic Goals and Milestones

In the dynamic world of ecommerce, success is often defined by the ability to set and achieve realistic goals and milestones. Clear objectives provide direction, motivation, and a framework for measuring progress. Whether you're launching a new ecommerce venture or looking to scale an existing business, here's a guide on how to set realistic goals and milestones:

Define Your Vision and Mission:

Vision: Clearly articulate the long-term vision for your ecommerce business.

Mission: Define the purpose and values that guide your business.

SMART Goal Framework:

Specific: Clearly define your goals with specific details.

Measurable: Establish metrics to track progress and success.

Achievable: Ensure that your goals are realistic and attainable.

Relevant: Align goals with your overall business strategy.

Time-bound: Establish precise due dates for finishing each task.

Categorize Goals:

Short-Term: Goals achievable within the next 6-12 months.

Mid-Term: Objectives that span 1-3 years.

Long-Term: Aspirations for the next 3-5 years or more.

Revenue and Sales Targets:

Breakdown: Set monthly and annual revenue targets.

Growth: Establish realistic growth percentages based on market analysis.

Customer Acquisition and Retention:

Acquisition: Set goals for increasing customer acquisition through marketing efforts.

Retention: Define strategies for retaining and nurturing existing customers.

Product and Service Expansion:

New Offerings: Set goals for introducing new products or services.

Diversification: Explore opportunities to enter new market segments.

Operational Efficiency:

Processes: Define goals for optimizing operational processes.

Resource Allocation: Ensure efficient use of resources for cost-effectiveness.

Market Share and Competitor Analysis:

Analysis: Set goals for gaining a specific percentage of market share.

Competitor Benchmarking: Compare your performance with key competitors.

Digital Presence and Marketing Goals:

Online Visibility: Set goals for improving online visibility through SEO and digital marketing.

Social Media Engagement: Define metrics for social media reach and engagement.

Customer Satisfaction and Feedback:

Surveys: Establish goals for customer satisfaction scores.

Feedback Loop: Regularly collect and analyze customer feedback for improvement.

Employee Development and Engagement:

Training Programs: Set goals for employee training and development.

Retention: Define strategies to enhance employee satisfaction and retention.

Risk Management and Contingency Planning:

Identify Risks: Set goals for identifying and mitigating potential risks.

Contingency Plans: Develop plans to address unforeseen challenges.

Collaboration and Partnerships:

Networking: Set goals for expanding industry connections.

Partnerships: Explore opportunities for strategic collaborations.

Financial Health:

Profitability: Set goals for achieving and maintaining profitability.

Budget Compliance: Monitor and control expenses to stay within budget.

Regular Review and Adaptation:

Review Periods: Schedule regular reviews of your goals and milestones.

Adaptability: Be willing to adjust goals based on market changes or unexpected circumstances.

Conclusion:

Setting realistic goals and milestones is not just about reaching destinations; it's about creating a journey that is purposeful, measurable, and adaptable. By aligning your goals with your vision and using the SMART framework, you lay the groundwork for a successful and sustainable ecommerce business. This book will guide you through the process of goal setting, providing insights and practical strategies to help you navigate the complexities of the ecommerce landscape and achieve your business objectives.

Chapter 4: Setting Up Your Home Ecommerce Office

Creating a Productive Workspace

The environment in which you work plays a pivotal role in your productivity, creativity, and overall well-being. Whether you're running an ecommerce business from home or managing a team in an office, optimizing your workspace is essential for achieving optimal performance. Here's a guide on creating a productive workspace:

Organize and Declutter:

Efficient Layout: Arrange furniture and equipment to create an efficient and ergonomic layout.

Declutter: Remove unnecessary items to reduce distractions and create a clean, organized space.

Ergonomic Furniture and Accessories:

Comfortable Seating: Invest in a comfortable chair with proper lumbar support.

Ergonomic Desk: Choose a desk at the right height to promote good posture.

Monitor Alignment: To lessen eye strain, align your computer monitor at eye level.

Natural Lighting:

Maximize Natural Light: Position your workspace near windows to benefit from natural light.

Adjustable Lighting: Use adjustable lighting to control brightness and reduce eye strain.

Personalization:

Inspiring Decor: Add decor that inspires and motivates you.

Personal Touch: Include personal items that make the space feel uniquely yours.

Technology Setup:

Efficient Equipment: Ensure your computer, printer, and other equipment are in good working order.

Cable Management: Keep cables organized to prevent tangling and tripping hazards.

Noise Control:

Noise-Canceling Headphones: Consider using noise-canceling headphones in a noisy environment.

Soundproofing: If possible, implement soundproofing measures to minimize external disturbances.

Task-Specific Zones:

Designate Areas: Create specific zones for different tasks (e.g., a focused work area, a collaboration zone).

Minimize Distractions: Keep non-essential items out of your primary workspace to minimize distractions.

Digital Organization:

File Management: Organize digital files into folders for easy retrieval.

Cloud Storage: Utilize cloud storage for accessibility and backup.

Plants and Greenery:

Natural Elements: Introduce plants or greenery to improve air quality and create a refreshing atmosphere.

Aesthetic Appeal: Plants can also add visual appeal to your workspace.

Comfortable Temperature:

Adjustable Thermostat: Ensure the workspace is at a comfortable temperature.

Ventilation: Good airflow is essential for maintaining a conducive work environment.

Inspiration Board:

Visual Goals: Create an inspiration board with images and quotes that align with your goals.

Motivational Element: This serves as a visual reminder of your aspirations.

Breakout Spaces:

Relaxation Area: If space allows, create a designated area for breaks and relaxation.

Mindfulness: Incorporate elements that encourage mindfulness and stress reduction.

Regular Maintenance:

Cleaning Schedule: Establish a regular cleaning and maintenance schedule.

Equipment Check: Ensure all equipment is in working order.

Communication Tools:

Efficient Tools: Utilize efficient communication tools for collaboration.

Virtual Meetings: Set up a dedicated area for virtual meetings with proper lighting and background.

Regular Evaluation and Adaptation:

Feedback Loop: Seek feedback on the workspace from yourself and others.

Adaptability: Be open to making adjustments based on changing needs and feedback.

Conclusion:

Creating a productive workspace is a dynamic process that requires attention to detail, regular evaluation, and adaptability. By incorporating ergonomic principles, optimizing your technology setup, and considering elements like lighting and organization, you can enhance your focus, creativity, and overall work satisfaction. This book will guide you through the steps of creating an efficient and inspiring workspace, ensuring that your environment supports your success in the dynamic world of ecommerce.

Essential Tools and Equipment

Running a successful ecommerce business requires the right set of tools and equipment to streamline operations, enhance efficiency, and provide a seamless customer experience. Whether you're a solo entrepreneur or managing a team, having the essential tools at your disposal is crucial. Here's a comprehensive guide to the essential tools and equipment for ecommerce:

Ecommerce Platform:

Examples: Shopify, WooCommerce, Magento, BigCommerce.

Purpose: Choose a user-friendly platform to build and manage your online store.

Website Hosting:

Examples: Bluehost, SiteGround, Shopify Hosting.

Purpose: Secure reliable hosting to ensure your website is accessible and performs well.

Domain Name:

Examples: GoDaddy, Namecheap.

Purpose: Register a memorable and brand-relevant domain name for your ecommerce site.

Payment Gateway:

Examples: PayPal, Stripe, Square.

Purpose: Enable secure online transactions by integrating a trusted payment gateway.

Customer Relationship Management (CRM):

Examples: HubSpot, Salesforce, Zoho CRM.

Purpose: Manage customer interactions, track leads, and enhance customer relationships.

Inventory Management:

Examples: TradeGecko, DEAR Inventory, Stitch Labs.

Purpose: Streamline inventory tracking, order fulfillment, and avoid stockouts.

Shipping and Logistics:

Examples: ShipStation, Shippo, Easyship.

Purpose: Simplify shipping processes, generate labels, and provide tracking information.

Ecommerce Analytics:

Examples: Google Analytics, Kissmetrics, Mixpanel.

Purpose: Track website traffic, customer behavior, and sales performance.

Email Marketing:

Examples: Mailchimp, Klaviyo, Constant Contact.

Purpose: Nurture customer relationships, send promotional campaigns, and automate email sequences.

Social Media Management:

Examples: Hootsuite, Buffer, Sprout Social.

Purpose: Schedule posts, monitor social media engagement, and analyze performance.

Content Management System (CMS):

Examples: WordPress, Joomla, Drupal.

Purpose: Manage and update website content easily without extensive technical knowledge.

Search Engine Optimization (SEO) Tools:

Examples: SEMrush, Moz, Ahrefs.

Purpose: Optimize your website for search engines, improve rankings, and drive organic traffic.

Customer Support and Live Chat:

Examples: Zendesk, LiveChat, Intercom.

Purpose: Provide real-time assistance, answer customer queries, and enhance customer support.

Security Software:

Examples: McAfee, Norton, Wordfence.

Purpose: Protect your website from cyber threats and ensure secure customer transactions.

Analytics and Reporting:

Examples: Google Analytics, Cyfe, Tableau.

Purpose: Generate comprehensive reports to assess business performance and make informed decisions.

Collaboration Tools:

Examples: Slack, Microsoft Teams, Trello.

Purpose: Facilitate communication and collaboration among team members.

Project Management:

Examples: Asana, Monday.com, Jira.

Purpose: Plan, track, and manage projects to ensure timely completion.

Graphic Design Tools:

Examples: Canva, Adobe Creative Cloud, PicMonkey.

Purpose: Create visually appealing product images, banners, and promotional material.

Mobile Optimization Tools:

Examples: Google Mobile-Friendly Test, AMP (Accelerated Mobile Pages).

Purpose: Ensure your website is optimized for mobile users.

Backup and Recovery Solutions:

Examples: UpdraftPlus, CodeGuard, Backblaze.

Purpose: Regularly back up your website data to prevent loss and facilitate recovery.

Conclusion:

Equipping your ecommerce business with the right tools and equipment is essential for staying competitive, managing operations efficiently, and delivering a positive customer experience. This guide provides a comprehensive overview, helping you select and integrate the essential tools that align with your business goals. As you navigate the ever-evolving landscape of ecommerce, these tools will serve as valuable assets in building and sustaining a successful online venture.

Legal and Regulatory Considerations

Launching and operating an ecommerce business involves navigating a complex landscape of legal and regulatory requirements. Ensuring compliance with these considerations is essential for the protection of your business, customers, and overall reputation. Here's a comprehensive guide on the key legal and regulatory considerations for ecommerce:

Business Structure and Registration:

Choose a Legal Structure: Decide on a business structure (e.g., sole proprietorship, LLC, corporation).

Register Your Business: Complete the necessary registration processes with relevant authorities.

Intellectual Property Protection:

Trademark Registration: Protect your brand by registering trademarks for your business name, logo, and products.

Copyright Protection: Secure copyright for original content, such as website text, images, and videos.

Data Protection and Privacy:

Privacy Policy: Clearly outline how customer data is collected, used, and protected in a privacy policy.

Compliance with Regulations: Adhere to data protection regulations such as GDPR (General Data Protection Regulation) or CCPA (California Consumer Privacy Act).

Terms of Service and User Agreements:

Terms and Conditions: Draft comprehensive terms of service outlining the rules and expectations for website users.

User Agreements: Establish user agreements to govern interactions on your platform.

Payment Card Industry Data Security Standard (PCI DSS) Compliance:

Secure Transactions: Ensure compliance with PCI DSS standards to secure customer payment information during transactions.

Online Sales Tax Compliance:

Understand Tax Obligations: Be aware of the tax implications and obligations for online sales in different jurisdictions.

Collect and Remit Taxes: Comply with applicable sales tax laws by collecting and remitting taxes as required.

Consumer Protection Laws:

Truth in Advertising: Adhere to truth in advertising laws, providing accurate and transparent information about products and services.

Product Liability: Be aware of product liability laws and ensure the safety and quality of products.

Electronic Contracts and Signatures:

Legally Binding Agreements: Ensure that electronic contracts and signatures are legally binding.

Adopt E-Signature Solutions: Implement secure e-signature solutions for online transactions.

Accessibility Compliance:

Web Content Accessibility Guidelines (WCAG): Ensure that your website complies with accessibility standards, making it accessible to individuals with disabilities.

Shipping and Fulfillment Compliance:

Shipping Regulations: Comply with shipping regulations and clearly communicate shipping terms and policies.

Customs and Import Laws: Understand and adhere to customs and import regulations for international shipments.

Age Verification and COPPA Compliance:

Age Restrictions: Implement age verification measures for products or services with age restrictions.

COPPA Compliance: Comply with the Children's Online Privacy Protection Act (COPPA) if targeting users under 13 years old.

Anti-Spam Regulations:

CAN-SPAM Act: Comply with the CAN-SPAM Act by providing opt-out options and truthful email content.

GDPR for Email Marketing: Adhere to GDPR regulations for email marketing if targeting European customers.

Affiliate Marketing Compliance:

Disclosure Requirements: Comply with disclosure requirements for affiliate marketing partnerships.

FTC Guidelines: Follow Federal Trade Commission (FTC) guidelines for transparency in endorsements and testimonials.

Compliance with Industry-Specific Regulations:

Industry Standards: Be aware of and comply with any industry-specific regulations relevant to your products or services.

Certifications: Obtain necessary certifications for specific industries, if applicable.

Dispute Resolution and Legal Jurisdiction:

Dispute Resolution Clauses: Include clear dispute resolution clauses in contracts and terms of service.

Legal Jurisdiction: Specify the legal jurisdiction in your terms to determine applicable laws in case of disputes.

Conclusion:

Prioritizing legal and regulatory compliance is fundamental to the success and longevity of your ecommerce business. Staying informed, seeking legal advice when needed, and proactively addressing these considerations contribute to building a trustworthy and legally sound online presence. This guide aims to provide a comprehensive overview, but it is crucial to consult with legal professionals to ensure compliance with specific regional and industry requirements. As you navigate the legal landscape, a well-informed and compliant approach will contribute to the growth and sustainability of your ecommerce venture.

Chapter 5: Building Your Ecommerce Website

Choosing the Right Ecommerce Platform

Selecting the right ecommerce platform is a critical decision that profoundly impacts the success and functionality of your online business. With a plethora of options available, each offering unique features and capabilities, it's essential to carefully evaluate your business needs, technical requirements, and long-term goals. Here's a comprehensive guide on how to choose the right ecommerce platform:

Define Your Business Requirements:

Product Type: Consider the nature of your products (physical, digital, services) and their variations.

Scalability: Assess your growth plans and ensure the platform can scale with your business.

Payment and Shipping Needs: Evaluate your preferred payment gateways, shipping options, and tax requirements.

Understand Your Technical Expertise:

Technical Skills: Assess your team's technical skills or your own capabilities.

Ease of Use: Choose a platform that aligns with your technical expertise, whether you're a beginner or an experienced developer.

Budget Considerations:

Platform Costs: Compare pricing models, including transaction fees, monthly subscriptions, and additional costs.

Scalability Costs: Consider how costs may change as your business grows.

Ecommerce Hosting:

Hosted vs. Self-Hosted: Decide between hosted solutions (e.g., Shopify) and self-hosted platforms (e.g., WooCommerce on WordPress).

Server Requirements: Ensure the platform is compatible with your preferred hosting service or comes with reliable hosting.

Mobile Responsiveness:

Mobile-Friendly Design: Choose a platform that offers responsive designs for optimal mobile user experiences.

Mobile App Support: Evaluate if the platform provides mobile apps or integrates well with third-party apps for on-the-go management.

Customization and Flexibility:

Theme Options: Assess the availability of customizable themes and templates.

Coding Capabilities: Determine if the platform allows for custom coding or if it has restrictions on modifications.

Ease of Integration:

Third-Party Integrations: Check the availability of integrations with essential tools and services (payment gateways, analytics, marketing tools).

API Access: Ensure the platform provides API access for custom integrations.

Security Features:

SSL Certification: Confirm the provision of SSL certification for secure data transmission.

Payment Security: Ensure compliance with PCI DSS standards for payment security.

SEO Friendliness:

SEO Tools: Look for built-in SEO tools or the ability to integrate with popular SEO plugins.

URL Structure: Ensure the platform allows for customizable and SEO-friendly URL structures.

Customer Support and Community:

Support Options: Evaluate the availability of customer support, including live chat, email, or phone support.

Community Forums: Check if the platform has an active community forum for user support and knowledge sharing.

Performance and Speed:

Loading Speed: Opt for a platform that offers fast loading times to enhance user experience.

Scalability Performance: Ensure the platform can handle traffic spikes without compromising performance.

Analytical Tools:

Built-In Analytics: Look for platforms with built-in analytics tools for tracking website performance.

Integration with External Analytics: Assess compatibility with external analytics tools such as Google Analytics.

Trial Periods and Demos:

Free Trials: Take advantage of free trial periods offered by many platforms.

Demos and Tutorials: Explore demo versions and tutorials to understand the platform's functionality.

Upgradability and Future-Proofing:

Software Updates: Check how regularly the platform receives updates.

Compatibility: Ensure the platform can adapt to future ecommerce trends and technological advancements.

Legal and Compliance Considerations:

Terms of Service: Review the platform's terms of service to ensure compliance with legal requirements.

Ownership and Data Control: Confirm your ownership and control over your data and content.

Conclusion:

Choosing the right ecommerce platform is a pivotal decision that shapes the foundation of your online business. By thoroughly evaluating your business needs, technical requirements, and future goals, you can make an informed decision that aligns with your vision. This guide provides a comprehensive checklist to guide you through the decision-making process, ensuring that the chosen platform not only meets your current needs but also supports the growth and success of your ecommerce venture.

Designing a User-Friendly Website

Creating a user-friendly website is crucial for providing a positive and engaging experience for your visitors. A well-designed website not only attracts users but also encourages them to stay longer, explore your content, and ultimately convert into customers. Here's a comprehensive guide on designing a user-friendly website:

Understand Your Target Audience:

User Persona: Develop user personas to understand the needs, preferences, and behaviors of your target audience.

User Journey: Map out the typical user journey from landing on the site to completing desired actions.

Clear and Intuitive Navigation:

Simple Menu Structure: Create a clear and concise menu structure for easy navigation.

Logical Hierarchy: Organize content with a logical hierarchy to guide users through the site seamlessly.

Mobile Responsiveness:

Responsive Design: Ensure your website is optimized for various devices, with a focus on mobile responsiveness.

Mobile-Friendly Features: Implement touch-friendly buttons and ensure readability on smaller screens.

Fast Loading Times:

Optimized photos: In order to speed up page loads, compress and optimize your photos.

Minimize Scripts: Limit the use of heavy scripts and plugins that can slow down the website.

Clear Call-to-Action (CTA):

Contrasting Buttons: Design CTA buttons with contrasting colors to make them stand out.

Compelling Copy: Use persuasive and action-oriented copy for your CTAs.

Intuitive Forms:

Simplified Fields: Keep forms concise with only essential fields to encourage user engagement.

Progress Indicators: If applicable, use progress indicators for multi-step forms to keep users informed.

Readable Typography:

Appropriate Font Sizes: Ensure text is easily readable with appropriately sized fonts.

Contrast: Use high contrast between text and background for optimal visibility.

Engaging Visuals:

High-Quality Images: Use high-quality and relevant images that enhance the visual appeal.

Infographics and Icons: Incorporate visual elements like infographics and icons to convey information succinctly.

Consistent Branding:

Logo Placement: Clearly display your logo in a consistent location throughout the site.

Color Palette: Maintain a consistent color palette and design elements that align with your brand.

Accessible Design:

Text for Images: Include descriptive alt text for images to aid users with visual impairments.

Keyboard Navigation: Ensure that all interactive elements can be navigated using a keyboard.

Search Functionality:

Prominent Search Bar: Place the search bar prominently for users seeking specific information.

Autocomplete and Suggestions: Implement autocomplete and suggestions to assist users during searches.

Feedback and Confirmation:

Form Validation: Provide real-time validation feedback for form entries to prevent errors.

Confirmation Messages: Clearly communicate successful actions with confirmation messages.

User-Friendly URLs:

Descriptive URLs: Create URLs that are descriptive and provide users and search engines with context.

Hierarchy: Use a clear hierarchy in URL structures to reflect the site's organization.

Social Media Integration:

Social Sharing Buttons: Include social sharing buttons for content dissemination.

Embedded Feeds: Embed social media feeds to showcase real-time engagement.

Regular Testing and Optimization:

A/B Testing: Conduct A/B testing for various elements to identify the most effective designs.

User Feedback: Gather user feedback and use analytics to continually optimize the user experience.

Conclusion:

Designing a user-friendly website is an ongoing process that involves understanding your audience, creating an intuitive navigation structure, and prioritizing user experience at every step. By implementing these best practices, you can create a website that not only attracts visitors but keeps them engaged and satisfied, fostering a positive relationship between your brand and your audience. This guide serves as a foundation for designing a user-friendly website that aligns with your business goals and enhances the overall online experience for your users.

Implementing Secure Payment Gateways

Ensuring the security of online transactions is a top priority for ecommerce businesses. Implementing secure payment gateways is crucial to protect sensitive customer information and build trust. Here's a comprehensive guide on how to implement secure payment gateways for your ecommerce platform:

Understand Payment Gateway Basics:

Definition: A payment gateway is a service that facilitates online transactions by securely transmitting payment information between the customer and the merchant.

Key Components: The gateway encrypts and authorizes payment details, ensuring a secure transfer of funds.

Compliance with PCI DSS Standards:

PCI DSS Definition: Payment Card Industry Data Security Standard (PCI DSS) is a set of security standards designed to ensure that all companies accepting, processing, storing, or transmitting credit card information maintain a secure environment.

Compliance Requirement: Choose a payment gateway provider that complies with PCI DSS standards.

Choose a Reputable Payment Gateway Provider:

Research: Investigate and choose a reputable payment gateway provider with a track record of security and reliability.

Customer Reviews: Consider customer reviews and testimonials regarding the provider's security measures.

Encryption Protocols:

SSL/TLS Encryption: Secure Sockets Layer (SSL) or Transport Layer Security (TLS) encryption should be implemented to secure data transmission between the customer's browser and the server.

Check for HTTPS: Ensure your website uses HTTPS to indicate a secure connection.

Tokenization:

Definition: Tokenization is the process of substituting sensitive data, like credit card numbers, with non-sensitive tokens.

Advantages: Reduces the risk of exposing sensitive information during transactions and storage.

Two-Factor Authentication (2FA):

Enhanced Security: Implement 2FA to add an extra layer of security, requiring users to provide two forms of identification before completing a transaction.

Customer Verification: Enhances the security of user accounts and transactions.

Fraud Detection and Prevention:

Real-Time Monitoring: Choose a payment gateway that offers real-time monitoring for unusual or suspicious activities.

Machine Learning: Implement machine learning algorithms to identify and prevent fraudulent transactions.

Payment Card Tokenization:

Secure Storage: If storing payment card information is necessary, use tokenization to securely store tokens instead of actual card numbers.

Minimize Data Exposure: Minimize the exposure of sensitive information to potential security threats.

Regular Security Audits:

Audit Procedures: Conduct regular security audits to identify and address potential vulnerabilities.

Penetration Testing: Perform penetration testing to simulate potential attacks and assess system resilience.

Customizable Security Settings:

Risk Thresholds: Choose a payment gateway that allows customization of risk thresholds to align with your business's risk tolerance.

Transaction Limits: Set transaction limits to prevent high-risk transactions.

Secure Customer Authentication (SCA):

EU Regulation: Comply with the Strong Customer Authentication requirements under the Payment Services Directive 2 (PSD2) in the European Union.

Multi-Factor Authentication: Implement multi-factor authentication for transactions in affected regions.

Educate Customers on Security Practices:

Clear Communication: Clearly communicate security measures and best practices to customers.

Phishing Awareness: Educate customers on recognizing phishing attempts to protect their personal information.

Payment Gateway Integration:

Seamless Integration: Ensure smooth integration of the payment gateway into your ecommerce platform.

Developer Support: Utilize developer support provided by the payment gateway for a secure implementation.

Continuous Monitoring and Updates:

Real-Time Monitoring: Continuously monitor transactions in real-time to detect and respond to security threats promptly.

Stay Updated: Keep the payment gateway software and security protocols up-to-date to address evolving threats.

Legal Compliance:

Terms and Conditions: Clearly outline payment terms and conditions in your website's policies.

Legal Compliance: Adhere to international and regional regulations governing online transactions.

Conclusion:

Implementing secure payment gateways is fundamental to safeguarding your ecommerce business and fostering customer trust. By adhering to industry standards, employing advanced security features, and staying informed about emerging threats, you can provide a secure and seamless payment experience for your customers. This guide serves as a comprehensive resource to help you navigate the intricacies of implementing secure payment gateways, protecting both your business and your customers from potential security risks.

Chapter 6: Sourcing Products and Inventory Management

Finding Reliable Suppliers

Securing reliable and trustworthy suppliers is a critical aspect of running a successful ecommerce business. The quality and reliability of your suppliers directly impact your product offerings, customer satisfaction, and overall business reputation. Here's a comprehensive guide on how to find reliable suppliers for your ecommerce venture:

Define Your Product Requirements:

Product Specifications: Clearly define the specifications, quality standards, and other requirements for the products you intend to source.

Quantity: Determine the quantity of products you need to source to meet market demand.

Research and Identify Potential Suppliers:

Industry Directories: Explore industry-specific directories and databases to identify potential suppliers.

Trade Shows and Exhibitions: Attend relevant trade shows and exhibitions to connect with suppliers in person.

Online Marketplaces: Utilize online platforms like Alibaba, ThomasNet, and other B2B marketplaces to discover suppliers.

Check Supplier Background and Reputation:

Company Background: Investigate the supplier's background, including their history, experience, and reputation in the industry.

Customer Reviews: Read customer reviews and testimonials to gauge the satisfaction of other businesses that have worked with the supplier.

Verify Legal and Compliance Aspects:

Legal Status: Confirm the legal status of the supplier, including business registration and compliance with industry regulations.

Product Compliance: Ensure that the supplier's products meet the necessary quality and safety standards.

Communication and Responsiveness:

Communication Channels: Assess the responsiveness and clarity of communication from potential suppliers.

Language Compatibility: Ensure effective communication by choosing suppliers with language compatibility.

Sample Product Testing:

Request Samples: Request samples of the products you plan to source to assess quality and consistency.

Quality Control Standards: Establish clear quality control standards and expectations.

Evaluate Production Capacity:

Scalability: Verify the supplier's production capacity to ensure they can meet your business's growth demands.

Lead Times: Inquire about lead times for production and shipping.

Financial Stability:

Financial Health: Assess the financial stability of potential suppliers to ensure their ability to fulfill orders consistently.

Payment Terms: Discuss and negotiate payment terms that align with your cash flow.

Supplier Certifications and Audits:

ISO Certifications: Check if the supplier holds relevant International Organization for Standardization (ISO) certifications.

Conduct Audits: Consider conducting on-site audits or hiring third-party auditing services for additional assurance.

Networking and Recommendations:

Industry Associations: Connect with industry associations and networks to get recommendations for reliable suppliers.

Peer Recommendations: Seek recommendations from other businesses in your industry.

Flexible Contract Terms:

Negotiate Terms: Negotiate flexible contract terms, including minimum order quantities, payment schedules, and delivery terms.

Legal Counsel: Consult legal counsel to ensure contracts protect your interests.

Diversification of Suppliers:

Risk Mitigation: Avoid dependence on a single supplier by diversifying your sources.

Backup Suppliers: Identify and establish relationships with backup suppliers to mitigate supply chain risks.

Transparent Pricing:

Detailed Cost Breakdown: Request a detailed breakdown of pricing, including production costs, shipping fees, and any additional charges.

Price Stability: Discuss strategies to maintain stable pricing over time.

Use Supplier Directories and Platforms:

Online Directories: Explore online supplier directories to find a variety of options.

Verified Platforms: Utilize verified supplier platforms that authenticate and verify supplier information.

Continuous Evaluation and Improvement:

Performance Metrics: Establish key performance indicators (KPIs) to regularly evaluate supplier performance.

Feedback Loop: Provide constructive feedback to suppliers and encourage open communication for continuous improvement.

Conclusion:

Building a network of reliable suppliers is a cornerstone of a successful ecommerce business. By conducting thorough research, assessing potential suppliers based on various criteria, and maintaining open communication, you can establish strong and enduring partnerships. This guide serves as a comprehensive resource to help you navigate the process of finding and partnering with reliable suppliers, ensuring the success and sustainability of your ecommerce venture.

Managing Inventory Efficiently

Efficient inventory management is crucial for the success of an ecommerce business. Striking the right balance between having enough stock to meet customer demand and avoiding excess inventory can significantly impact your bottom line. Here's a comprehensive guide on how to manage inventory efficiently:

Implement an Inventory Management System:

Choose a Suitable System: Invest in a robust inventory management system that aligns with the size and complexity of your business.

Automation Features: Leverage automation features for tasks such as order tracking, stock level updates, and reordering.

Categorize Inventory:

ABC Analysis: Categorize products using the ABC analysis (Class A for high-value items, Class B for moderate, and Class C for low).

Seasonal Classification: Identify and categorize products based on seasonal demand patterns.

Set Reorder Points and Safety Stock:

Reorder Point: Determine the minimum stock level at which you should reorder products.

Safety Stock: Maintain a safety stock to account for unexpected demand spikes or delays from suppliers.

Real-Time Tracking and Reporting:

Utilize Technology: Employ real-time tracking tools to monitor inventory levels, sales trends, and order fulfillment.

Customizable Reports: Generate customizable reports to analyze inventory turnover, stockouts, and excess inventory.

Forecast Demand Accurately:

Historical Data Analysis: Use historical sales data to forecast demand accurately.

Market Trends: Stay informed about market trends and external factors that may impact demand.

Optimize Order Quantities:

Economic Order Quantity (EOQ): Calculate the EOQ to determine the optimal order quantity that minimizes holding and ordering costs.

Batch Ordering: Consolidate orders to reduce shipping and handling costs.

Supplier Relationship Management:

Regular Communication: Maintain open communication with suppliers to stay informed about lead times, potential delays, and production schedules.

Negotiate Favorable Terms: Negotiate favorable terms such as bulk discounts and flexible payment schedules.

Implement FIFO and LIFO:

FIFO (First In, First Out): Prioritize selling the oldest inventory first to prevent obsolescence.

LIFO (Last In, First Out): Use LIFO for perishable goods or when newer inventory is more desirable.

Cycle Counting and Audits:

Regular Cycle Counts: Conduct regular cycle counts to reconcile physical inventory with recorded levels.

Audits: Perform occasional audits to ensure accuracy and identify discrepancies.

Integrate with Sales Channels:

Automated Integration: Integrate your inventory management system with sales channels to automatically update stock levels after each sale.

Multi-Channel Selling: Manage inventory efficiently across multiple platforms with centralized control.

Implement Just-In-Time (JIT) Inventory:

Reduce Holding Costs: Adopt JIT inventory practices to minimize holding costs by receiving goods only when needed.

Supplier Collaboration: Collaborate closely with suppliers for timely deliveries.

Utilize Barcoding and RFID Technology:

Barcoding: Implement barcoding systems for accurate tracking and efficient order processing.

RFID (Radio-Frequency Identification): Explore RFID technology for real-time inventory tracking and management.

Streamline Returns and Exchanges:

Efficient Returns Process: Develop a streamlined returns process to quickly reintegrate returned items into inventory.

Quality Control: Inspect returned items for quality to prevent restocking damaged goods.

Cross-Functional Collaboration:

Collaborative Teams: Encourage collaboration between sales, marketing, and inventory management teams to share insights and align strategies.

Regular Meetings: Conduct regular cross-functional meetings to address challenges and optimize processes.

Continuous Improvement:

Regular Review: Regularly review and adjust inventory management strategies based on changing market conditions and business goals.

Feedback Loop: Encourage feedback from team members involved in inventory management for continuous improvement.

Conclusion:

Efficient inventory management is a dynamic process that requires a combination of technology, strategic planning, and continuous improvement. By implementing the right tools and practices, staying informed about market trends, and fostering strong relationships with suppliers, you can maintain optimal inventory levels, reduce costs, and enhance overall business efficiency. This guide provides a comprehensive framework to help you navigate the complexities of managing inventory efficiently in the ever-evolving landscape of ecommerce.

Implementing Dropshipping Strategies

Dropshipping is a popular ecommerce fulfillment method that allows businesses to sell products without holding inventory. Rather, goods are sent straight from suppliers to clients. Successfully implementing dropshipping strategies requires careful planning, reliable partnerships, and effective management. Here's a comprehensive guide on how to implement dropshipping strategies for your ecommerce business:

Selecting Niche and Products:

Niche Selection: Identify a specific niche or market segment that aligns with your business goals and target audience.

Product Research: Choose products with high demand, low competition, and reasonable profit margins.

Research and Choose Reliable Suppliers:

Supplier Verification: Thoroughly research and verify the reliability of potential suppliers.

Communication: Establish clear communication channels with suppliers to ensure efficient order processing.

Build a Robust Ecommerce Platform:

Choose a Suitable Platform: Select an ecommerce platform that supports dropshipping integrations and provides the necessary features.

User-Friendly Design: Optimize your website for user-friendliness, with clear navigation and compelling product displays.

Integrate with Dropshipping Platforms:

Use Established Platforms: Integrate with established dropshipping platforms like Oberlo, Spocket, or AliExpress.

Automation: Leverage automation tools to streamline order processing and inventory management.

Pricing and Profit Margins:

Competitive Pricing: Set competitive prices to attract customers while maintaining healthy profit margins.

Factor in Costs: Consider product costs, shipping fees, and any additional expenses when determining prices.

Transparent and Clear Policies:

Shipping Policies: Clearly communicate shipping times, tracking information, and any potential delays to customers.

Return and Refund Policies: Establish transparent return and refund policies to manage customer expectations.

Quality Control and Product Testing:

Order Samples: Purchase samples from suppliers to assess product quality and shipping times.

Quality Assurance: Implement quality control measures to ensure customers receive satisfactory products.

Marketing and Branding:

Unique Selling Proposition (USP): Develop a unique value proposition that distinguishes your brand from competitors.

Content Marketing: Create engaging content that highlights product benefits and educates customers.

Customer Service Excellence:

Responsive Support: Provide responsive customer support to address inquiries, concerns, and issues promptly.

Clear Communication: Communicate transparently about shipping times and product availability.

Optimize for Search Engines (SEO):

Keyword Optimization: Optimize product listings and content for relevant keywords to improve search engine rankings.

High-Quality Images and Descriptions: Use high-quality images and detailed product descriptions to enhance SEO.

Monitor and Manage Inventory:

Regular Inventory Checks: Regularly monitor inventory levels and update product availability on your website.

Automated Updates: Use automation tools to update inventory in real-time based on supplier information.

Scaling and Diversification:

Explore New Products: Continuously explore new products and suppliers to diversify your product offerings.

Expand Marketing Channels: Consider expanding to new marketplaces and channels for increased visibility.

Secure Payment Processing:

Reliable Payment Gateways: Choose reliable and secure payment gateways to ensure smooth transactions.

Offer Multiple Payment Options: Provide customers with various payment options for flexibility.

Legal Compliance:

Terms of Service: Clearly outline terms of service, shipping policies, and return conditions on your website.

Legal Consultation: Consult legal professionals to ensure compliance with regulations in your target markets.

Continuous Optimization and Adaptation:

Analytical Tools: Use analytics tools to gather insights into customer behavior, sales trends, and website performance.

Adaptation: Continuously optimize your dropshipping strategies based on data, market changes, and customer feedback.

Conclusion:

Implementing dropshipping strategies requires a well-thought-out plan, reliable partnerships, and a commitment to customer satisfaction. By carefully selecting products, establishing transparent policies, and leveraging technology for automation, you can build a successful dropshipping business. This guide provides a comprehensive framework to help you navigate the intricacies of implementing effective dropshipping strategies for your ecommerce venture.

Chapter 7: Marketing Your Ecommerce Business

Developing a Comprehensive Marketing Plan

A well-thought-out marketing strategy is necessary for any firm to succeed. It serves as a roadmap to reach and engage your target audience, build brand awareness, and drive sales. Here's a comprehensive guide on how to develop a marketing plan that aligns with your business goals:

Define Your Business Objectives:

SMART Goals: Clearly outline Specific, Measurable, Achievable, Relevant, and Time-bound goals for your marketing efforts.

Business Alignment: Ensure that your marketing objectives align with the overall business objectives.

Know Your Target Audience:

Customer Persona Development: Create detailed customer personas based on demographics, psychographics, and behavior.

Segmentation: Identify and segment your target audience to tailor marketing strategies for specific groups.

Conduct a SWOT Analysis:

Strengths and Weaknesses: Assess internal factors, including strengths and weaknesses within your business.

Opportunities and Threats: Analyze external factors, identifying opportunities and potential threats in the market.

Understand the Marketing Mix (4Ps):

Product: Define your product or service offerings and their unique selling points.

Price: Establish pricing strategies based on market research, competition, and perceived value.

Place: Determine the distribution channels and locations where your products or services will be available.

Promotion: Develop strategies for promoting your offerings through advertising, public relations, and other channels.

Create a Budget:

Allocate Resources: Determine the budget for each marketing initiative, considering both online and offline channels.

ROI Expectations: Set clear expectations for return on investment (ROI) from each marketing channel.

Choose Marketing Channels:

Digital Channels: Select online channels such as social media, email marketing, content marketing, and search engine optimization (SEO).

Traditional Channels: Consider traditional channels like print, radio, TV, and direct mail, depending on your target audience.

Develop a Content Strategy:

Content Calendar: Create a content calendar outlining the type and frequency of content for various channels.

Value Proposition: Ensure that your content communicates a clear value proposition and resonates with your target audience.

Social Media Marketing:

Platform Selection: Choose social media platforms based on your target audience's preferences and behaviors.

Engagement Strategies: Develop strategies for engaging your audience through regular posts, contests, and interactive content.

Email Marketing:

Segmentation: Segment your email list for personalized and targeted campaigns.

Automation: Utilize email automation for welcome sequences, drip campaigns, and follow-ups.

Search Engine Optimization (SEO):

Keyword Research: To improve the content of your website, do extensive keyword research.

On-Page and Off-Page Optimization: Implement both on-page and off-page SEO strategies to improve search engine rankings.

Paid Advertising:

PPC Campaigns: Set up pay-per-click (PPC) advertising campaigns on platforms like Google Ads and social media.

Ad Creatives: Create compelling ad creatives with clear calls-to-action.

Public Relations and Influencer Marketing:

Media Relationships: Cultivate relationships with relevant media outlets for press coverage.

Influencer Partnerships: Collaborate with influencers who align with your brand values and target audience.

Measure and Analyze Results:

Key Performance Indicators (KPIs): Define KPIs such as website traffic, conversion rates, social media engagement, and sales.

Analytics Tools: Use analytics tools to track and measure the performance of each marketing channel.

Feedback Mechanism:

Customer Feedback: Gather feedback from customers through surveys, reviews, and social media interactions.

Internal Evaluation: Conduct internal assessments to gather insights from your team's perspective.

Adapt and Refine:

Continuous Improvement: Continuously analyze results and adapt your marketing strategies based on performance.

Market Trends: Stay informed about industry trends and adjust your plan to stay competitive.

Conclusion:

A comprehensive marketing plan serves as a dynamic guide for achieving your business objectives and staying ahead in a competitive landscape. By understanding your audience, utilizing various marketing channels, and regularly analyzing performance, you can create a plan that adapts to market changes and drives sustained business growth. This guide provides a foundational framework to help you develop a marketing plan tailored to your business needs and goals.

Utilizing Social Media Marketing

Businesses may now effectively engage with their audience, increase brand exposure, and foster participation through social media. Effectively utilizing social media marketing can enhance your online presence and contribute to business growth. Here's a comprehensive guide on how to harness the power of social media for your marketing strategy:

Define Your Social Media Goals:

Brand Awareness: Increase visibility and recognition for your brand.

Engagement: Foster meaningful interactions with your audience.

Lead Generation: Capture and nurture potential leads.

Sales: Drive revenue through social media channels.

Choose the Right Social Media Platforms:

Know Your Audience: Select platforms where your target audience is most active.

Platform Features: Consider the features and strengths of each platform (e.g., visual content on Instagram, professional networking on LinkedIn).

Create a Consistent Brand Identity:

Visual Elements: Maintain a consistent visual theme, including logo, colors, and imagery.

Voice and Tone: Develop a consistent voice and tone in your content that aligns with your brand personality.

Content Strategy and Planning:

Content Calendar: Plan and schedule posts in advance with a content calendar.

Varied Content Types: Share a mix of visuals, videos, articles, and user-generated content to keep your feed diverse and engaging.

Engage with Your Audience:

Respond Promptly: Respond to comments, messages, and mentions promptly to foster engagement.

Ask Questions: Encourage conversations by asking questions and seeking feedback.

Incorporate Visual Content:

High-Quality Images and Graphics: Use visually appealing images and graphics to capture attention.

Videos and Live Streams: Leverage video content, including live streams, for higher engagement.

Hashtag Strategies:

Brand-Specific Hashtags: Create and promote branded hashtags for user-generated content.

Trending Hashtags: Participate in relevant trending hashtags to increase discoverability.

Run Contests and Giveaways:

Increase Engagement: Contests and giveaways encourage audience participation and sharing.

Set Clear Rules: Clearly outline rules, timelines, and prizes to avoid confusion.

Utilize Influencer Marketing:

Identify Relevant Influencers: Collaborate with influencers whose audience aligns with your target market.

Authentic Partnerships: Encourage authentic collaborations that resonate with both the influencer and your brand.

Social Media Advertising:

Targeted Ads: Use targeted advertising to reach specific demographics and interests.

Ad Formats: Experiment with various ad formats, such as carousel ads, stories, and sponsored posts.

Analytics and Insights:

Platform Analytics: Utilize built-in analytics tools on platforms like Facebook Insights, Instagram Insights, and Twitter Analytics.

Third-Party Tools: Consider using third-party analytics tools for more in-depth analysis.

Community Building:

Create Groups or Communities: Foster a sense of community by creating groups or communities related to your brand.

User-Generated Content: Inspire customers to talk about their interactions with your goods and services.

Stay Informed about Trends:

Algorithm Changes: Stay updated on platform algorithm changes to adjust your strategy accordingly.

Emerging Features: Try out the newest functionalities that social media networks have to offer.

Collaborate with Other Brands:

Cross-Promotions: Collaborate with complementary brands for cross-promotions.

Co-Branded Campaigns: Launch co-branded campaigns for mutual benefits.

Legal and Ethical Considerations:

Data Privacy: Adhere to data privacy regulations and protect user information.

Transparent Disclosures: Clearly disclose partnerships, sponsored content, and any potential conflicts of interest.

Conclusion:

The field of social media marketing is dynamic and always changing. By understanding your goals, choosing the right platforms, and consistently engaging with your audience, you can leverage social media to build a strong brand presence, foster community, and achieve your business objectives. This guide serves as a foundational resource to help you harness the full potential of social media marketing for your brand.

Search Engine Optimization (SEO) Strategies

SEO is crucial for enhancing online visibility and driving organic traffic to your website. Employing effective SEO strategies ensures that your content is easily discoverable by search engines and, consequently, by your target audience. Here's a comprehensive guide on how to implement SEO strategies to improve your website's ranking:

Keyword Research:

Determine Relevant Keywords: To identify keywords that are pertinent to your business, use tools such as Google Keyword Planner.

Long-Tail Keywords: Target long-tail keywords for specific and niche-focused content.

On-Page SEO Optimization:

Optimize Title Tags: Create compelling and keyword-rich title tags for each page.

Meta Descriptions: Write concise meta descriptions that encourage clicks and include relevant keywords.

URL Structure: Keep URLs short, descriptive, and include target keywords.

Header Tags: Use header tags (H1, H2, H3) to structure content and highlight important information.

Optimize Images: Use informative alt text and reduce file size for quicker page loads.

Quality Content Creation:

Relevant and Informative Content: Create content that is relevant, informative, and valuable to your target audience.

Content-Length: Aim for comprehensive content when appropriate, but prioritize quality over quantity.

Regular Updates: Keep your content updated and relevant to maintain search engine rankings.

Mobile Optimization:

Mobile-Friendly Design: Ensure your website is mobile-friendly for a positive user experience.

Responsive Design: Use responsive design to adapt to various screen sizes.

Page Loading Speed:

Optimize Images: Compress images without compromising quality to improve loading speed.

Reduce the amount of components on a page that call for different server queries by minimising the number of HTTP requests.

Technical SEO:

XML Sitemap: Create and submit an XML sitemap to search engines for easy indexing.

Robots.txt: Make the file as efficient as possible to direct search engine crawlers regarding which pages to index.

Canonical URLs: To prevent problems with duplicating material, use canonical tags.

Link Building:

Quality Backlinks: Focus on acquiring high-quality, relevant backlinks from reputable websites.

Internal Linking: Implement internal linking to guide users and search engines to relevant content within your site.

Social Media Integration:

Social Signals: Optimize your social media profiles and encourage sharing to boost social signals.

Linking Social Profiles: Link your social media profiles to your website for cross-platform visibility.

Local SEO Optimization:

Google My Business: Claim and optimize your Google My Business listing for local searches.

Local Citations: Make sure all online directories have up-to-date business information.

User Experience (UX):

Intuitive Navigation: Create a user-friendly website with intuitive navigation.

Readability: Use legible fonts and proper formatting for an easy reading experience.

Monitor and Analyze:

Google Analytics: Set up Google Analytics to track website traffic, user behavior, and other crucial metrics.

Search Console: Utilize Google Search Console to monitor site performance, fix issues, and submit sitemaps.

Content Diversification:

Video Content: Incorporate video content as it has become increasingly favored by search engines.

Infographics and Images: Use visually appealing content like infographics to diversify your content.

Voice Search Optimization:

Natural Language Keywords: Optimize for natural language queries as voice search continues to rise.

FAQ Sections: Include FAQ sections to answer common questions users may ask through voice search.

Regular SEO Audits:

Identify Issues: Conduct regular SEO audits to identify and address technical issues and opportunities.

Competitor Analysis: Monitor competitors and adjust your strategies based on industry trends.

Adapt to Algorithm Changes:

Stay Informed: Keep up-to-date with search engine algorithm changes and adjust your strategies accordingly.

White-Hat Techniques: Focus on ethical, white-hat SEO techniques to maintain long-term success.

Conclusion:

Implementing effective SEO strategies is an ongoing process that requires a combination of technical expertise, content creation, and adaptability to industry changes. By focusing on the key elements outlined in this guide, you can enhance your website's visibility, attract a larger audience, and ultimately improve your online presence. This comprehensive approach to SEO will help your website rank higher in search engine results and drive sustained organic traffic.

Chapter 8: Customer Service Excellence

Providing Outstanding Customer Support

Exceptional customer support is a cornerstone of successful businesses, fostering customer loyalty, positive reviews, and long-term relationships. Here's a comprehensive guide on how to provide outstanding customer support that exceeds expectations:

Responsive Communication:

Timely Responses: Respond promptly to customer inquiries, whether through email, chat, or phone.

24/7 Accessibility: If feasible, offer round-the-clock customer support or clearly communicate your service hours.

Empathy and Understanding:

Listen Actively: Pay attention to customer concerns and inquiries, demonstrating that their opinions matter.

Empathize: Understand the customer's perspective and express empathy towards their situation.

Knowledgeable Support Team:

Comprehensive Training: Ensure your support team is well-trained on products, services, and common customer issues.

Continuous Learning: Regularly update your team on new features, updates, and industry trends.

Multi-Channel Support:

Omni-Channel Approach: Provide support across various channels, including email, phone, live chat, and social media.

Unified Experience: Ensure a consistent and seamless experience regardless of the channel customers choose.

Personalized Assistance:

Use Customer Data: Leverage customer data to personalize interactions and provide more relevant assistance.

Recognize Returning Customers: Acknowledge and appreciate repeat customers to build a sense of familiarity.

Clear and Concise Communication:

Avoid Jargon: Communicate in simple, easy-to-understand language, avoiding technical jargon.

Transparency: Clearly explain processes, policies, and resolutions to customers.

Proactive Problem Resolution:

Anticipate Issues: Identify potential problems and proactively address them before they escalate.

Provide Solutions: Offer solutions rather than just acknowledging problems, demonstrating a commitment to resolution.

Feedback Collection:

Surveys and Feedback Forms: Gather customer feedback through surveys to understand their experiences.

Monitor Online Reviews: Keep track of online reviews and address both positive and negative feedback.

Self-Service Options:

Knowledge Base: Develop a comprehensive knowledge base or FAQ section to empower customers to find answers independently.

Tutorials and Guides: Provide instructional content, such as video tutorials or step-by-step guides.

Fast Issue Resolution:

First-Contact Resolution: Strive to resolve issues during the first customer contact whenever possible.

Escalation Process: Have a clear process for escalating complex issues to higher-tier support if necessary.

Customer Education:

Educational Content: Share educational content to help customers make the most of your products or services.

Webinars or Workshops: Conduct webinars or workshops to deepen customer understanding.

Appreciation and Rewards:

Loyalty Programs: Implement loyalty programs or exclusive offers to reward repeat customers.

Express Appreciation: Thank customers for their business and express gratitude for their loyalty.

Continuous Improvement:

Feedback Analysis: Analyze customer feedback to identify recurring issues and areas for improvement.

Employee Feedback: Gather insights from your support team to refine processes and enhance service quality.

Crisis Management:

Prepare for Crises: Develop a crisis management plan to handle unexpected challenges or service interruptions.

Transparent Communication: Communicate openly and transparently during crises, keeping customers informed.

Empowerment of Frontline Staff:

Decision-Making Authority: Empower frontline support staff to make decisions and resolve issues without unnecessary escalations.

Continuous Training: Provide ongoing training to ensure staff is equipped to handle various scenarios.

Conclusion:

Outstanding customer support is a strategic investment that pays dividends in customer satisfaction, loyalty, and positive word-of-mouth. By prioritizing responsive communication, empathy, and continuous improvement, businesses can build strong relationships with their customers and differentiate themselves in a competitive market. This guide serves as a foundation for creating a customer-centric support strategy that elevates the overall customer experience.

Handling Returns and Resolving Issues

Dealing with returns and resolving issues is an integral part of providing excellent customer service. How a business manages these situations can significantly impact customer satisfaction and loyalty. Here's a comprehensive guide on how to handle returns and effectively resolve customer issues:

Clear and Transparent Return Policy:

Clearly communicate your return policy on your website and during the purchasing process.

Make the policy easily accessible, detailing conditions, timeframes, and procedures.

Streamlined Return Process:

Simplify the return process to reduce customer effort.

Provide a user-friendly online return portal or clear instructions for in-store returns.

Prompt and Responsive Communication:

Acknowledge return requests promptly, assuring customers that their concerns are being addressed.

Maintain open communication channels via email, chat, or phone.

Empathetic Customer Interaction:

Train customer support staff to handle return requests with empathy and understanding.

Express genuine concern for the customer's inconvenience and dissatisfaction.

No-Hassle Refunds and Exchanges:

Process refunds or exchanges quickly without unnecessary delays.

Minimize bureaucratic steps and paperwork, making the process hassle-free.

Prepaid Return Labels:

Provide prepaid return labels to simplify the return shipping process.

Absorb or clearly communicate any associated return shipping costs.

Automated Return Updates:

Implement automated systems to update customers on the status of their return.

Send confirmation emails upon receiving the returned item and processing the refund or exchange.

Root Cause Analysis:

Investigate the reasons behind returns to identify patterns or product/service issues.

Use this analysis to make informed decisions on product improvements or service enhancements.

Customer Education on Products:

Offer detailed product descriptions and specifications to set accurate customer expectations.

Provide resources such as guides, tutorials, or FAQs to address common product-related issues.

Flexible Solutions:

- Be flexible in finding solutions, offering alternatives like exchanges, store credit, or discounts.

- Consider case-by-case assessments for unique situations.

Escalation Procedures:

- Establish clear procedures for escalating complex issues to higher tiers of support.

- Ensure that frontline support staff can efficiently communicate with higher-level teams.

Documentation of Returns:

- Maintain thorough records of return transactions, reasons, and resolutions.

- Use this data for trend analysis and continuous improvement.

Proactive Issue Resolution:

- Anticipate potential issues by monitoring customer feedback and product performance.

- Proactively address issues before they lead to a surge in returns.

Post-Resolution Follow-Up:

- Follow up with customers after the resolution to ensure their satisfaction.

- Use feedback to enhance processes and prevent similar issues in the future.

Employee Empowerment:

- Empower customer support staff to make decisions within predefined guidelines.

- Train staff to handle irate or frustrated customers with professionalism and patience.

Conclusion:

Efficiently handling returns and resolving customer issues is an opportunity to turn a potentially negative experience into a positive one. By being transparent, responsive, and empathetic, businesses can not only retain customers but also build trust and loyalty. This guide provides a foundation for creating a customer-centric approach to returns and issue resolution, emphasizing the importance of continuous improvement and proactive customer support.

Building Customer Loyalty

Customer loyalty is the cornerstone of a successful and sustainable business. Cultivating a loyal customer base not only drives repeat business but also enhances brand advocacy and positive word-of-mouth. Here's a comprehensive guide on how to build and foster customer loyalty:

Exceptional Customer Service:

Responsive Support: Provide timely and effective customer support to address queries and concerns.

Personalized Interactions: Tailor interactions to each customer, showing that their needs are understood and valued.

Consistent Brand Experience:

Uniform Branding: Maintain a consistent brand image across all touchpoints, from online presence to in-store experiences.

Consistent Messaging: Ensure that your brand messaging aligns with your values and resonates with your target audience.

Loyalty Programs:

Reward Systems: Implement loyalty programs with incentives, discounts, or exclusive access for repeat customers.

Tiered Rewards: Create tiered programs that encourage customers to reach higher levels for increased benefits.

Personalized Marketing:

Data Utilization: Leverage customer data to create personalized marketing campaigns.

Segmentation: Segment your customer base to send targeted and relevant messages.

Quality Products and Services:

Consistent Quality: Deliver products or services of consistent high quality to meet or exceed customer expectations.

Continuous Improvement: Seek feedback and continually improve your offerings based on customer input.

Customer Feedback and Surveys:

Feedback Channels: Create avenues for customers to provide feedback, such as surveys or reviews.

Act on Feedback: Actively use customer feedback to make improvements and show that their opinions matter.

Exclusive Access and Previews:

VIP Access: Provide loyal customers with exclusive access to new products, services, or promotions.

Sneak Previews: Offer early previews or launches for your loyal customer base.

Social Media Engagement:

Community Building: Foster a sense of community on social media platforms, encouraging customers to engage with each other and your brand.

Respond Promptly: Respond promptly to comments, mentions, and messages, showing that you value online interactions.

Surprise and Delight:

Unexpected Rewards: Occasionally surprise customers with unexpected rewards, discounts, or personalized gifts.

Birthday and Anniversary Recognition: Acknowledge and celebrate customers' special occasions with personalized messages or offers.

Transparency and Trust:

Transparent Communication: Build trust by being transparent about your products, services, and policies.

Honesty in Marketing: Avoid misleading marketing tactics and be truthful in all communications.

Consistent Engagement:

Regular Communication: Keep customers engaged through regular newsletters, updates, or informative content.

Interactive Content: Create interactive content that encourages participation and involvement.

Easy and Seamless Transactions:

User-Friendly Interfaces: Ensure that your website or app provides a seamless and easy shopping experience.

Efficient Checkout Process: Streamline the checkout process to reduce friction.

Customer Education Programs:

Product Knowledge: Offer resources, tutorials, or webinars to educate customers about your products or services.

Problem-Solving Guides: Provide guides to help customers troubleshoot common issues.

Flexibility and Adaptability:

Flexible Policies: Be flexible with policies, especially in unique or challenging situations.

Adapt to Customer Needs: Adapt your offerings or services based on changing customer needs and preferences.

Employee Training and Alignment:

Customer-Centric Culture: Instill a customer-centric culture within your organization through employee training and alignment.

Frontline Empowerment: Empower frontline staff to make decisions that prioritize customer satisfaction.

Conclusion:

Building customer loyalty is an ongoing process that requires a holistic approach, focusing on customer experience, value, and engagement. By consistently delivering exceptional service, personalizing interactions, and rewarding customer loyalty, businesses can create lasting connections that go beyond transactions. This guide provides a foundational framework for fostering customer loyalty and building a customer base that not only stays but becomes advocates for your brand.

Chapter 9: Scaling Your Ecommerce Business

Analyzing Data and Making Informed Decisions

In the digital age, businesses have access to a wealth of data that, when properly analyzed, can provide valuable insights for strategic decision-making. Here's a comprehensive guide on how to analyze data effectively and use it to make informed decisions for the success of your business:

Define Clear Objectives:

Clearly outline the objectives you want to achieve through data analysis.

Align data analysis goals with overall business goals to ensure relevance.

Data Collection and Organization:

Identify relevant data sources, including customer interactions, sales, website analytics, and market trends.

Organize data systematically, ensuring it is accurate, up-to-date, and stored securely.

Choose the Right Analytics Tools:

Select analytics tools that align with your data analysis needs and technical capabilities.

Utilize a combination of tools for different types of data, such as Google Analytics, Excel, or specialized business intelligence platforms.

Data Cleaning and Preprocessing:

Cleanse data of errors, duplicates, and outliers to ensure accuracy.

Preprocess data for consistency and compatibility across various sources.

Data Visualization:

Use visualizations like charts, graphs, and dashboards to make complex data more understandable.

Visualization aids in spotting trends, patterns, and outliers.

Identify Key Performance Indicators (KPIs):

Define and prioritize KPIs that directly impact business objectives.

Regularly monitor KPIs to gauge performance and identify areas for improvement.

Perform Descriptive Analysis:

Summarize and describe the main features of the dataset.

Identify trends, patterns, and anomalies through descriptive statistics.

Conduct Diagnostic Analysis:

Explore relationships within the data to understand cause-and-effect dynamics.

Use diagnostic analysis to uncover factors influencing specific outcomes.

Predictive Modeling:

Employ predictive analytics to forecast future trends or outcomes.

Use machine learning algorithms for more accurate predictions, especially in areas like customer behavior or market demand.

Segmentation and Targeting:

- Segment your audience or market based on relevant criteria.

- Tailor marketing strategies and offerings to specific segments for greater effectiveness.

Customer Journey Analysis:

- Map the customer journey to understand touchpoints, pain points, and opportunities for improvement.

- Optimize customer experience based on insights gained from the analysis.

Competitor Analysis:

- Analyze competitor data to benchmark performance and identify areas of competitive advantage.

- Keep up with advancements and trends in the industry.

Social Media Listening:

- Utilize social media listening tools to analyze customer sentiments and feedback.

- Respond to customer concerns and leverage positive feedback for marketing.

Cost-Benefit Analysis:

- Evaluate the costs and benefits associated with various business initiatives.

- Prioritize projects with a favorable cost-benefit ratio for resource allocation.

Continuous Monitoring and Iteration:

- Implement a system for continuous data monitoring and analysis.

- Iterate on strategies based on real-time data to adapt to changing market conditions.

Data Security and Compliance:

- Prioritize data security and ensure compliance with relevant regulations (e.g., GDPR, HIPAA).

- Implement robust cybersecurity measures to protect sensitive information.

Collaboration Across Teams:

- Foster collaboration between data analysts, decision-makers, and relevant departments.

- Share insights and encourage cross-functional discussions.

Training and Skill Development:

- Invest in training for employees involved in data analysis.

- Keep teams updated on the latest tools, methodologies, and industry best practices.

Ethical Considerations:

- Consider ethical implications when collecting and analyzing data.

- Ensure that data practices align with ethical standards and respect user privacy.

Document Decision-Making Processes:

- Maintain clear documentation of the decision-making process.

- Document assumptions, methodologies, and key insights to facilitate future analysis and learning.

Conclusion:

Analyzing data is a powerful tool for making informed decisions that can drive business success. By establishing clear objectives, employing the right tools, and fostering a data-driven culture within your organization, you can leverage data to gain a competitive edge, enhance customer experiences, and adapt to the dynamic landscape of the business environment. This guide provides a foundational framework for effectively analyzing data and translating insights into strategic actions.

Expanding Product Lines and Market Reach

Expanding your product lines and reaching new markets are essential strategies for business growth. By diversifying your offerings and tapping into new customer segments, you can increase revenue and establish a more resilient business. Here's a comprehensive guide on how to successfully expand your product lines and market reach:

Market Research and Analysis:

Identify Market Gaps: Conduct thorough market research to identify gaps or unmet needs in your current market.

Analyze Competitors: Study competitors' product lines and market strategies to uncover potential opportunities.

Customer Segmentation:

Understand Target Audiences: Segment your existing and potential customer base to understand their preferences and needs.

Tailor Offerings: Develop products that cater to the specific demands of different customer segments.

Product Development Strategy:

Innovate Existing Products: Enhance and innovate your current product offerings to keep them competitive.

Introduce New Products: Introduce entirely new products that complement or expand upon your existing lineup.

Quality Assurance and Testing:

Ensure Product Quality: Maintain high-quality standards for new and existing products.

Conduct Testing: Thoroughly test new products before launch to identify and address any potential issues.

Brand Consistency:

Maintain Brand Cohesion: Ensure that new products align with your brand identity and values.

Consistent Messaging: Maintain consistent messaging across all products to reinforce brand recognition.

E-Commerce and Online Presence:

Optimize E-Commerce Platforms: Leverage online channels to reach a wider audience.

Implement SEO Strategies: Optimize product listings for search engines to enhance online visibility.

Partnerships and Collaborations:

Strategic Partnerships: Form partnerships with other businesses to expand distribution channels.

Collaborative Products: Collaborate with other brands to create unique, co-branded products.

International Expansion:

Market Analysis: Evaluate international markets to identify opportunities and challenges.

Adapt to Local Preferences: Tailor products to meet the specific preferences and cultural nuances of target international markets.

Franchising and Licensing:

Explore Franchising: Consider franchising your business model to enter new markets.

Licensing Agreements: License your brand or products to partners who can introduce them to different regions.

Customer Feedback and Testing:

Beta Testing: Engage in beta testing with a select group of customers to gather feedback.

Iterative Improvement: Use customer feedback to iteratively improve products before full-scale launch.

Pricing Strategies:

Competitive Pricing: Price products competitively in each target market.

Bundle Offers: Consider bundling products for enhanced value and customer appeal.

Supply Chain Optimization:

Scalable Supply Chains: Ensure your supply chain is scalable to meet increased demand.

Local Sourcing: Optimize supply chain logistics to support international expansion.

Marketing and Promotion:

Localized Marketing: Tailor marketing strategies to resonate with the culture and preferences of different markets.

Digital Marketing Campaigns: Leverage digital channels for targeted advertising to reach specific demographics.

Regulatory Compliance:

Understand Local Regulations: Be aware of and comply with regulations in new markets.

Product Certifications: Obtain necessary certifications to meet local standards and requirements.

Employee Training and Cultural Awareness:

Cultural Sensitivity: Train employees to be culturally sensitive when entering new markets.

Language Proficiency: Ensure that staff can communicate effectively in languages relevant to target markets.

Customer Education:

Educational Content: Provide educational resources to familiarize customers with new product features.

Interactive Demonstrations: Conduct product demonstrations or webinars to showcase benefits.

Feedback Loops and Iteration:

Continuous Feedback: Establish feedback loops to gather ongoing insights from customers.

Iterative Improvement: Use feedback to iterate on products and strategies for continuous improvement.

Monitoring and Analytics:

Performance Metrics: Establish key performance indicators (KPIs) to monitor the success of new product launches.

Analytics Tools: Utilize analytics tools to track customer behavior, sales, and market trends.

Risk Assessment and Mitigation:

Conduct Risk Analysis: Identify potential risks associated with market expansion.

Mitigation Strategies: Develop mitigation strategies to address identified risks proactively.

Legal Considerations:

Intellectual Property Protection: Ensure that your intellectual property is protected in new markets.

Legal Compliance: Understand and comply with local laws and regulations related to product offerings.

Conclusion:

Successfully expanding product lines and market reach requires a strategic and well-executed approach. By understanding your target audiences, innovating products, and adapting to diverse market dynamics, you can position your business for sustained growth. This guide provides a comprehensive framework for navigating the complexities of expansion, ensuring that your efforts are informed, strategic, and aligned with your overall business goals.

Hiring Help and Outsourcing Tasks

As businesses grow, the demand for diverse skills and expertise often surpasses the capacity of existing teams. To manage workloads efficiently and maintain focus on core competencies, many businesses turn to hiring help and outsourcing tasks. Here's a comprehensive guide on how to effectively hire external assistance and outsource tasks to enhance productivity and achieve business goals:

Identify Areas for Outsourcing:

Assess Workload: Identify tasks or projects that can be delegated without compromising quality.

Define Core Competencies: Focus on outsourcing non-core functions to free up resources for strategic priorities.

Define Clear Objectives:

Set Specific Goals: Clearly define what you aim to achieve through outsourcing.

Measurable Metrics: Establish measurable metrics to evaluate the success of outsourced tasks.

Cost-Benefit Analysis:

Evaluate Costs: Compare the costs of outsourcing versus hiring additional in-house resources.

Factor in Quality: Consider the potential improvement in task quality when assessing overall value.

Outsourcing Partners Selection:

Research Potential Partners: Thoroughly research and vet potential outsourcing partners.

Check References: Obtain and verify references to gauge the reliability and reputation of outsourcing vendors.

Legal Agreements and Contracts:

Detailed Contracts: Draft comprehensive contracts that clearly define tasks, expectations, and deliverables.

Legal Consultation: Seek legal advice to ensure contracts protect your interests and comply with relevant regulations.

Effective Communication:

Regular Updates: Establish a communication plan with regular updates and progress reports.

Responsive Communication: Encourage open communication channels to address queries or concerns promptly.

Data Security and Confidentiality:

Ensure Data Protection: Implement robust data security measures to protect sensitive information.

Confidentiality Agreements: Require outsourcing partners to sign confidentiality agreements to safeguard proprietary data.

Start with Small Projects:

Pilot Projects: Begin with smaller projects to test the capabilities and reliability of outsourcing partners.

Scale Gradually: Gradually increase the scale of outsourced tasks as trust is established.

Training and Onboarding:

Provide Clear Guidelines: Offer detailed guidelines and training materials to ensure understanding.

Onboarding Process: Facilitate a smooth onboarding process for external teams to align with your business practices.

Monitor Performance Metrics:

Key Performance Indicators (KPIs): Establish KPIs to monitor the performance of outsourced tasks.

Regular Evaluation: Conduct regular evaluations to ensure alignment with objectives.

Flexibility and Adaptability:

Adapt to Changes: Be flexible in adapting to changes in the outsourcing landscape.

Feedback Integration: Incorporate feedback from both internal and external teams for continuous improvement.

Cultural Sensitivity:

Understand Cultural Differences: Consider cultural nuances when working with outsourcing partners from different regions.

Build Cultural Bridges: Foster a collaborative environment that bridges cultural gaps for effective teamwork.

In-House Team Collaboration

Communication Channels: Establish efficient communication channels between in-house and outsourced teams.

Regular Meetings: Conduct regular virtual or in-person meetings to maintain alignment and collaboration.

Scalability Planning:

Anticipate Growth: Plan for scalability to accommodate increased outsourcing needs.

Flexible Agreements: Ensure contracts have provisions for scaling up or down based on business requirements.

Risk Mitigation:

Identify Risks: Conduct a thorough risk assessment and identify potential challenges.

Mitigation Strategies: Develop strategies to mitigate identified risks and challenges proactively.

Quality Control Measures:

Quality Assurance Processes: Implement robust quality control measures to maintain high standards.

Regular Audits: Conduct periodic audits to ensure compliance with quality expectations.

Customer Service Excellence:

Aligned Service Standards: Ensure that outsourced customer service aligns with your brand's service standards.

Customer Feedback Integration: Integrate customer feedback to refine and improve outsourced service.

Employee Morale and Management:

Transparent Communication: Communicate the benefits of outsourcing transparently to internal teams.

Address Concerns: Address any concerns or fears among existing employees regarding job security.

Continuous Evaluation and Improvement:

Feedback Loops: Establish feedback loops to gather insights from both internal and external stakeholders.

Iterative Improvement: Use feedback to iteratively improve processes and collaboration.

Long-Term Relationship Building:

Invest in Relationships: Cultivate strong, long-term relationships with outsourcing partners.

Collaborative Growth: Work collaboratively to ensure mutual growth and success.

Conclusion:

Hiring help and outsourcing tasks can be a strategic move for businesses looking to optimize resources and focus on core competencies. By carefully selecting partners, fostering effective communication, and maintaining a commitment to quality, businesses can achieve successful outcomes through outsourcing. This guide provides a comprehensive framework to navigate the complexities of outsourcing and ensure that it contributes positively to overall business objectives.

Chapter 10: Financial Management and Quitting Your Day Job

Setting Financial Goals and Budgeting

Establishing clear financial goals and implementing an effective budget are fundamental steps towards achieving financial success and stability. Whether you're managing personal finances or steering a business, a well-thought-out plan can provide direction, discipline, and a roadmap for future growth. Here's a comprehensive guide on setting financial goals and creating a robust budget:

Identify Short-Term and Long-Term Goals:

Short-Term Goals: Define achievable goals within the next 6-12 months.

Long-Term Goals: Outline objectives that span multiple years, such as buying a home or retirement planning.

Prioritize Your Goals:

Critical Priorities: Identify the most pressing financial goals that require immediate attention.

Sequential Planning: Prioritize goals in a logical sequence, considering dependencies and timelines.

Make Goals SMART:

Specific: State your goals in unambiguous terms.

Measurable: Define metrics to track progress.

Achievable: Set realistic goals within your current means.

Relevant: Ensure goals align with your overall financial vision.

Time-Bound: Assign deadlines to create a sense of urgency.

Personal Finance Goals:

Emergency Fund: Set a goal for creating and maintaining an emergency fund.

Debt Repayment: Prioritize paying off high-interest debts.

Savings for Specific Purchases: Plan for significant expenses like a new vehicle or a vacation.

Business Finance Goals:

Profitability: Set targets for increasing profitability and maintaining positive cash flow.

Investment: Establish goals for business expansion, product development, or technology upgrades.

Debt Management: Plan for reducing business debts and optimizing interest payments.

Budgeting Basics:

Income Analysis: Identify all income sources, including wages, business revenue, and investments.

Expense Breakdown: Categorize and list all monthly expenses, distinguishing between fixed and variable costs.

Create a Realistic Budget:

Track Historical Spending: Analyze past spending patterns to inform your budget.

Account for All Expenses: Consider often overlooked expenses like subscriptions, maintenance, and irregular bills.

Allocate for Savings:

Pay Yourself First: Allocate a portion of your income for savings before covering other expenses.

Automate Savings: Set up automated transfers to savings accounts for consistency.

Debt Repayment Plan:

Prioritize High-Interest Debt: Allocate extra funds to pay off high-interest debts first.

Snowball Method: Consider the debt snowball method for psychological wins by paying off smaller debts first.

Review and Adjust Regularly:

Monthly Review: Regularly review your budget to ensure alignment with financial goals.

Adjust as Necessary: Modify the budget based on changing circumstances or unexpected expenses.

Emergency Fund:

Establish Fund Size: Aim to build an emergency fund that covers 3-6 months of living expenses.

Consistent Contributions: Regularly contribute to the emergency fund, even when focusing on other financial goals.

Investment and Retirement Planning:

Diversified Investments: Diversify your investment portfolio based on risk tolerance and financial goals.

Regular Contributions: Consistently contribute to retirement accounts, taking advantage of employer matches if applicable.

Insurance Coverage:

Assess Coverage Needs: Regularly reassess insurance needs for health, life, property, and business.

Optimize Policies: Ensure policies align with current circumstances and offer adequate coverage.

Tax Planning:

Understand Tax Implications: Be aware of tax implications for personal and business income.

Leverage Tax Benefits: Explore tax-advantaged savings and investment options.

Education and Skill Development Budget:

Allocate for Learning: Dedicate a portion of your budget for ongoing education and skill development.

Invest in Growth: Consider courses or workshops that enhance personal or professional capabilities.

Celebrate Milestones:

Acknowledge Achievements: Celebrate reaching financial milestones, whether paying off a debt or achieving a savings goal.

Reward Yourself: Consider small rewards to maintain motivation and discipline.

Financial Advisor Consultation:

Professional Guidance: Seek advice from financial advisors for personalized insights and strategies.

Regular Check-Ins: Schedule periodic consultations to align your financial plan with changing circumstances.

Financial Literacy and Awareness:

Educate Yourself*:* Stay informed about financial trends, investment strategies, and economic indicators.

Regular Reading*:* Incorporate financial literature into your regular reading habits.

Financial Wellness Check:

Periodic Assessments: Conduct financial wellness check-ins to evaluate overall financial health.

Adjust Goals: Modify financial goals based on evolving priorities and circumstances.

Crisis and Contingency Planning:

Emergency Protocols*:* Establish crisis management protocols for unforeseen financial challenges.

Contingency Fund: Maintain a contingency fund within your budget for unexpected expenses.

Conclusion:

Setting financial goals and implementing a well-structured budget are integral components of achieving financial stability and success. By aligning your aspirations with realistic objectives, creating a disciplined budget, and regularly reassessing your financial plan, you can navigate the complexities of personal and business finance effectively. This guide provides a comprehensive framework to empower you in taking control of your financial journey and working towards a secure and prosperous future.

Knowing When It's Time to Quit Your Day Job

Deciding to transition from a traditional job to pursue entrepreneurship or alternative career paths is a significant and life-altering decision. Recognizing the right time to quit your day job requires careful evaluation of various factors to ensure a smooth and successful transition. Here's a comprehensive guide on how to identify when it's the appropriate moment to make the leap:

Financial Preparedness:

Sufficient Savings: Ensure you have a robust financial cushion, including an emergency fund, to cover living expenses for an extended period.

Stable Income Stream: If possible, establish a stable income stream from your new venture or alternative sources.

Business Viability:

Positive Business Indicators: Observe positive signs in your entrepreneurial endeavor, such as growing customer base, consistent revenue, and market demand.

Business Plan Validation: Validate your business plan through successful pilot projects or initial product/service launches.

Clear Business Vision:

Defined Business Goals: Have a clear understanding of your business goals, target audience, and revenue projections.

Sustainable Model: Ensure your business has a sustainable and scalable model that aligns with your long-term vision.

Market Validation:

Positive Feedback: Gather positive feedback and testimonials from early customers or clients.

Market Research: Validate your business concept through thorough market research, indicating a demand for your product or service.

Passion and Commitment:

Passionate Engagement: Feel a deep sense of passion and commitment to your new venture.

Willingness to Invest Time: Be prepared to invest significant time and effort into your business, especially during the initial stages.

Assessment of Personal Goals:

Alignment with Personal Aspirations: Ensure that quitting your day job aligns with your personal and professional aspirations.

Balance of Risk and Reward: Assess the risks involved against the potential rewards and personal fulfillment.

Health and Well-Being:

Manageable Stress Levels: Evaluate your stress levels and overall well-being in your current job.

Positive Impact on Health: Consider how the transition may positively impact your physical and mental health.

Opportunities for Growth:

Stagnation at Current Job: If your current job offers limited opportunities for growth and advancement, it may be a signal to explore new avenues.

Learning and Skill Development: Assess if your entrepreneurial pursuit provides opportunities for continuous learning and skill development.

Support System:

Emotional Support: Have a strong support system, including friends, family, or mentors, who understand and encourage your decision.

Professional Guidance: Seek advice from professionals or mentors in your industry for insights and guidance.

Timeline and Milestones:

Established Timeline: Set a realistic timeline for quitting your day job based on achieving specific milestones.

Measurable Progress: Regularly evaluate progress towards these milestones to gauge your readiness.

Network and Connections:

Industry Relationships: Cultivate a network within your industry that can provide support, collaboration, and potential business opportunities.

Professional Alliances: Identify alliances and partnerships that can enhance your entrepreneurial journey.

Legal and Contractual Considerations:

Review Employment Contracts: If applicable, review employment contracts and non-compete agreements to ensure compliance.

Legal Consultation: Seek legal advice to navigate any legal considerations associated with leaving your current job.

Timing in Economic Conditions:

Economic Stability: Consider the overall economic conditions and stability when contemplating the transition.

Industry Trends: Be aware of trends in your industry that may impact the success of your venture.

Personal and Professional Development:

Continuous Learning: Embrace a mindset of continuous learning and development.

Skill Enhancement: Focus on acquiring skills that will contribute to your success in the new venture.

Feedback from Advisors:

Mentor Feedback: Seek feedback from mentors or advisors who can offer an objective perspective.

Adaptability Recommendations: Assess recommendations on your adaptability to the challenges of entrepreneurship.

Business Stability:

Consistent Revenue: Achieve consistent revenue streams that can sustain your lifestyle.

Operational Stability: Ensure operational stability and efficiency within your business.

Work-Life Balance:

Improved Balance: Evaluate if quitting your day job will contribute to a healthier work-life balance.

Quality of Life: Consider how the change may positively impact your overall quality of life.

Exit Strategy:

Clearly Defined Exit Strategy: Have a clearly defined exit strategy from your current job.

Smooth Transition Plan: Develop a plan to ensure a smooth transition for both you and your employer.

Risk Tolerance:

Understanding Risks: Assess your risk tolerance and willingness to navigate the uncertainties of entrepreneurship.

Risk Mitigation Strategies: Develop strategies to mitigate potential risks and challenges.

Reflect on Personal Values:

Alignment with Values: Reflect on whether your current job aligns with your personal values.

Entrepreneurial Alignment: Ensure that your new venture resonates with your values and principles.

Conclusion:

Deciding when to quit your day job is a highly personal and strategic choice. By evaluating financial readiness, business viability, personal goals, and various other factors, you can make an informed decision that aligns with your aspirations. This guide provides a comprehensive framework to guide your decision-making process, ensuring a smooth transition into the next phase of your professional journey.

Making the Transition Smoothly

Transitioning from one phase of your professional journey to another, such as moving from a traditional job to entrepreneurship or a new career path, requires careful planning and execution to ensure a smooth and successful shift. Here's a comprehensive guide on how to make the transition smoothly:

Thorough Planning:

Create a Transition Plan: Develop a detailed plan outlining the steps and milestones for your transition.

Timeline: Establish a realistic timeline, considering both short-term and long-term goals.

Financial Preparation:

Maintain Financial Stability: Ensure you have sufficient savings to cover living expenses during the transition period.

Emergency Fund: Have a robust emergency fund to address unexpected financial challenges.

Business Readiness:

Validate Business Model: Validate your business model through market research and pilot projects.

Operational Efficiency: Ensure your business operations are streamlined and efficient.

Build a Support System:

Professional Advisors: Seek guidance from mentors, advisors, and professionals in your industry.

Personal Support: Cultivate a strong personal support system to provide emotional encouragement.

Maintain a Work-Life Balance:

Prioritize Well-Being: Emphasize the importance of maintaining a healthy work-life balance.

Self-Care: Incorporate self-care practices to manage stress and maintain well-being.

Legal and Contractual Considerations:

Review Contracts: Carefully review employment contracts and legal obligations.

Seek Legal Advice: Consult with a legal professional to ensure a smooth exit from your current job.

Effective Communication:

Notify Employers Professionally: Inform your employer of your decision professionally and with ample notice.

Transparent Communication: Communicate transparently with colleagues about your transition plans.

Skill Enhancement:

Continuous Learning: Continue enhancing your skills through courses or workshops.

Stay Updated: Stay abreast of industry trends and innovations.

Networking and Relationship Building:

Professional Networking: Cultivate relationships within your industry for support and collaboration.

Maintain Connections: Keep in touch with former colleagues and industry peers.

Set Clear Business Objectives:

Define Clear Goals: Clearly outline your business objectives and strategies.

Measurable Targets: Establish measurable targets for business growth and success.

Adaptability and Flexibility:

Adapt to Changes: Be adaptable to unexpected challenges and changes.

Flexibility in Plans: Allow for flexibility in your plans to accommodate unforeseen circumstances.

Technology Integration:

Leverage Technology: Utilize technology to enhance business processes and communication.

Digital Presence: Establish a strong online presence for your business.

Professional Development:

Continuous Improvement: Commit to continuous professional development.

Industry Involvement: Participate in industry events and forums to stay connected.

Delegate Responsibilities:

Effective Delegation: Delegate tasks efficiently within your business.

Empower Your Team: Ensure your team is empowered to handle responsibilities in your absence.

Customer Transition Plan:

Communicate with Clients: Communicate changes to your clients or customers transparently.

Ensure Continuity: Develop a plan to ensure continuity of service during the transition.

Create a Contingency Plan:

Identify Potential Risks: Anticipate potential risks and challenges during the transition.

Mitigation Strategies: Develop strategies to mitigate identified risks.

Celebrate Achievements:

Acknowledge Milestones: Celebrate achievements, both personal and professional.

Reflect on Progress: Take time to reflect on the progress you've made.

Evaluate and Adjust:

Periodic Reviews: Conduct periodic reviews of your transition plan.

Adjust Strategies: Adjust strategies based on evolving circumstances and lessons learned.

Maintain Professionalism:

Professional Image: Maintain a professional image during and after your transition.

Positive Reputation: Uphold a positive reputation within your industry.

Seek Feedback:

Feedback Loops: Create feedback loops to ensure ongoing development.

Learn from Experiences: Use feedback to learn from your experiences and refine your approach.

Conclusion:

Making a smooth transition requires a holistic and strategic approach, encompassing financial preparation, effective communication, skill enhancement, and ongoing evaluation. By diligently planning, staying adaptable, and building a strong support system, you can navigate the complexities of transition with confidence. This guide provides a comprehensive framework to guide you through the process, ensuring a seamless move towards your new professional journey.

Conclusion

Celebrating Your Ecommerce Success

Embarking on the journey of building and growing an ecommerce business is a remarkable endeavor that demands dedication, resilience, and strategic planning. As you reach the conclusion of this exciting phase and reflect on your achievements, it's essential to take a moment to celebrate the milestones and successes that define your ecommerce venture.

The path to success in the ecommerce realm is multifaceted, involving meticulous market research, a deep understanding of your audience, and the implementation of innovative strategies. From identifying profitable niches to crafting a unique brand identity, you've navigated through challenges, adapted to market trends, and worked tirelessly to establish a thriving online presence.

Celebrate the Growth:

Take pride in the growth and expansion of your ecommerce business. Whether you've increased your product offerings, expanded your market reach, or witnessed a surge in customer engagement, each accomplishment contributes to the overall success of your venture. Acknowledge the efforts that have propelled your business forward and recognize the impact you've made in the digital marketplace.

Appreciate Customer Loyalty:

The heart of any successful ecommerce business lies in its ability to cultivate and maintain a loyal customer base. Take a moment to appreciate the trust your customers have placed in your brand. Whether through exceptional customer service, quality products, or engaging marketing campaigns, your ability to foster lasting relationships is a testament to your dedication to customer satisfaction.

Reflect on Lessons Learned:

In the dynamic world of ecommerce, every challenge and setback presents an opportunity for learning and improvement. Reflect on the lessons gained from both successes and failures. Whether refining your marketing strategy, optimizing the user experience, or adapting to industry trends, the insights gained along the way contribute to the continuous evolution of your business.

Express Gratitude:

Your ecommerce success is not a solitary achievement but a collaborative effort involving the support of various stakeholders. Express gratitude to your team, partners, and customers who have played pivotal roles in your journey. Recognize the collective contributions that have propelled your business to new heights and celebrate the collaborative spirit that defines your ecommerce community.

Plan for the Future:

As you celebrate your current success, set your sights on the future. Consider new opportunities for growth, innovative strategies to stay ahead of the competition, and ways to further enhance the customer experience. A forward-thinking mindset will position your ecommerce business for sustained success in the ever-evolving digital landscape.

In conclusion, celebrating your ecommerce success is not just about acknowledging achievements; it's about recognizing the collective efforts, learning from experiences, and expressing gratitude for the journey. Your ecommerce venture is a dynamic, evolving entity, and each celebration marks a milestone on the path to greater heights. May your continued dedication and strategic vision lead to even more remarkable accomplishments in the vibrant world of ecommerce. Cheers to your success!

Looking Ahead: Continuous Growth and Innovation

As we conclude our exploration of the dynamic landscape of continuous growth and innovation, it's evident that the journey toward success is an ongoing evolution in the ever-changing realms of business and technology. Embracing the spirit of adaptability, foresight, and creativity, we recognize that the pursuit of excellence is not a destination but a perpetual quest for improvement.

In the realms of business, staying relevant requires a commitment to continuous growth and innovation. From the inception of new ideas to the implementation of cutting-edge technologies, the ability to evolve and adapt is paramount. As we look ahead, the horizon is filled with opportunities for those willing to embrace change and push the boundaries of conventional thinking.

Continuous Growth:

The essence of continuous growth lies not only in scaling operations but also in the relentless pursuit of improvement. It involves refining processes, expanding knowledge, and cultivating a mindset that values learning from every experience. Whether through exploring untapped markets, diversifying product offerings, or enhancing operational efficiency, the journey of growth is a perpetual one.

Innovation as a Driving Force:

Innovation serves as the catalyst for transformative change. It is the driving force behind breakthroughs, new products, and revolutionary processes. By fostering a culture of innovation within your organization, you empower your team to think creatively, challenge the status quo, and contribute to the development of solutions that redefine industry standards.

Technological Advancements:

In the fast-paced world of business, technology is a key driver of innovation. From artificial intelligence and machine learning to blockchain and augmented reality, advancements in technology offer unprecedented possibilities for businesses to streamline operations, enhance customer experiences, and gain a competitive edge. Embracing these technologies positions businesses to navigate the future landscape with agility.

Adapting to Market Dynamics:

Market dynamics are inherently fluid, influenced by economic shifts, consumer behaviors, and global events. Successful businesses recognize the importance of staying attuned to these dynamics and adapting strategies accordingly. Whether through market research, trend analysis, or customer feedback, the ability to pivot in response to changing conditions is a hallmark of sustained success.

Investing in People:

Every successful endeavor has a group of committed people at its core. Investing in the growth and development of your team members fosters a culture of collaboration and shared success. As we look ahead, nurturing talent, providing opportunities for skill development, and fostering a positive work environment become integral components of sustained growth.

Environmental and Social Responsibility:

In an era where social and environmental responsibility are paramount, businesses are increasingly recognizing the importance of contributing to positive change. Sustainability, ethical practices, and social impact initiatives not only align with societal expectations but also resonate with an ever-conscious consumer base.

In conclusion, the path forward is illuminated by the twin beacons of continuous growth and innovation. As we navigate the complexities of the future, let us embrace change as an opportunity, celebrate diversity as a strength, and forge ahead with a commitment to making a positive impact. The journey of growth and innovation is not just about reaching new heights; it's about shaping a future that is dynamic, inclusive, and filled with possibilities. May your endeavors be marked by resilience, creativity, and a relentless pursuit of excellence in the exciting chapters that lie ahead.

www.ingramcontent.com/pod-product-compliance
Lightning Source LLC
Chambersburg PA
CBHW081202290526
45796CB00010B/316